COLLIER QUICK AND EASY SERIES

SKIING WITH CONTROL

IMPROVE PRACTICAL OR VOCATIONAL SKILLS
SUPPLEMENT YOUR FORMAL EDUCATION
GET MORE FUN OUT OF HOBBIES

This Collier guide is designed to offer concise, authoritative information in a clear, readable manner. Carefully prepared with the latest, up-to-the-minute material, it is also valuable as a source for permanent reference. Titles in the Quick and Easy series include—

AMERICAN HISTORY
Robert Sobel, Ph.D.

ARITHMETIC
Simon Dresner

BOOKKEEPING
Morton D. Bluestone, M.A.

BOWLING
Hal and Jean Vermes

BUSINESS LETTER WRITING
Abraham Ellenbogen

CARPENTRY
Clarence Herisko

CHESS
Richard Roberts

DRIVING
Edward A. McInroy, M.A.

ECONOMICS
*George G. Dawson, Ph.D.,
and Russell H. McClain, Ph.D.*

EFFECTIVE SPEAKING
Bernice Loren

ELECTRONICS
Jesse Dilson

ETIQUETTE
Dorothy Sara

FAMILY CAMPING
William P. Luce

GOLF
Robert Scharff

HI FI AND STEREO
Richard Roberts

HOME MAINTENANCE
Martin Sara

HOME NURSING CARE
*Lucille Gidseg, R.N.,
and Dorothy Sara*

HUNTING
Robert Scharff

INSURANCE
Martin Cornwall

LAW
Jesse Raphael, LL.B.

MAGIC
Hal G. Vermes

MAKING HOME MOVIES
Bob Knight

MOTOR BOATING
Robert Scharff

PHYSICAL FITNESS
Justus Schifferes, Ph.D.

PLAYING THE GUITAR
Frederick M. Noad

RAPID READING
*Myron Q. Herrick, The
Reading Laboratory, Inc.*

RUNNING A MEETING
Jack T. Parker

SALESMANSHIP
Hal G. Vermes

SEWING
Dorothy Stepat De Van

SKIING WITH CONTROL
*Rick Shambroom
and Betty Slater*

TENNIS
Robert Scharff

TV WRITING
George Lowther

WATER SKIING
Glen E. Anderson

WORLD HISTORY
Edwin Dunbaugh, Ph.D.

COLLIER QUICK AND EASY SERIES

SKIING WITH CONTROL

*A Self-Instruction Guide to Techniques
and Equipment — Developed, Tested and
Perfected Throughout the Major
Skiing Countries of the World*

BY RICK SHAMBROOM & BETTY SLATER

PHOTOGRAPHS BY DAVID BLUMENTHAL ASSOCIATES

COLLIER BOOKS, NEW YORK / COLLIER-MACMILLAN LTD., LONDON

A COLLIER BOOKS ORIGINAL

First Edition 1965

The Macmillan Company, New York
Collier-Macmillan Ltd., Toronto, Ontario
Printed in the United States of America

CONTENTS

FOREWORD

SKIING IS FUN from the very beginning. If you do nothing more than put on a pair of skis and walk around a golf course, you'll come back invigorated. It's that kind of sport. But the real sense of exhilaration and feelings of accomplishment come with your ability to ski down a slope under full control. The greater your control of the skis, the more fun you have. The relationship is direct. This book will help you learn to control your skis.

Whether you are a beginner, an intermediate, or an advanced skier, if you read each section carefully, study the illustrations, and practice the exercises, your skiing will improve. For you have already shown, by picking up this book, that you possess the first essential: the desire to learn. Skiing is easy for anyone who really wants to learn and is willing to practice.

Next you need competent instruction. The best way to get it is to take a week or two of consecutive lessons in a certified ski school. However, you may be one of the many people who would like to do this but can't. Maybe you are planning to take classes but you want to know what it's all about before you go; or perhaps you've already taken lessons and now want to continue to progress. In any case, if you are eager to learn, this book is written specifically for you. You'll find that it is a simplified explanation of the modern method of skiing, rather than a technical treatise. There's an easy-to-grasp explanation of the principles of skiing, a graphic description of body movement, step-by-step suggestions for practice, plus a wealth of tricks and insights gathered from instructors all over the ski world.

There are many different theories and successful methods of teaching skiing. You won't get bogged down in a discussion of their relative merits here. What we are setting forth is the best of several techniques—a combination of ideas developed, tested, and perfected by ski school directors, Olympic champions, and seasoned professionals throughout the United States, Canada, and Europe. Although skiing is a dynamic sport and the methods of teaching it are constantly being revised, we are presenting the most up-to-date thinking and ideas which will help you regardless of where you go skiing.

Skiing is an expression of individual personality and physical build. No two people have exactly the same bone structure and muscular development; nor do they think alike. Yet everyone can use the same principles of skiing. This leads to individuality of style. For instance, six instructors teaching in the same ski school come down the mountain skiing the same technique. Despite the precision of identical movements, you can distinguish each one by his own particular style. The overall plan in this book will aid you to develop your own style within the framework of your build and interest.

There was a time when we would not have attempted to teach you to ski through the pages of a book. But it has become apparent that you do learn more quickly when you understand what it is you're trying to do, and why. The learning process is more than just watching and imitating, although this can surely be beneficial if you're watching a "pro." But even when you are observing an instructor, this aspect of learning will be more meaningful when you know what to look for. The purpose of this book is to give you that understanding easily and quickly, so that you can go out onto the slopes and practice, confident that you will progress.

There were two pitfalls we tried to avoid. One

was to be so technical that each section would be loaded down with insignificant details, giving you the impression that learning to ski is an impossibly difficult, dull task. It isn't.

The opposite extreme was to be so brief that we would fail to give you sufficient information and word pictures to be of real help in teaching you. We steered a middle road.

Certain concepts and descriptions seem to be repetitious. This emphasis is deliberate, for there are principles you'll be exposed to early in the book which are the basis for more advanced skiing. They are repeated and stressed at all stages where they apply.

This book was designed to be used. Read over the instructions the night before you go skiing. Read them again in the morning before you actually start up the slope. In this way, your understanding of the movements will be fresh in your mind and your learning time will be shortened.

Naturally, the more you practice, the sooner you'll achieve your goal. For it takes practice—lots of it —to absorb, master, and incorporate these skiing concepts into your own experience. And if you can

practice under the guidance of a certified instructor, so much the better.

Any book such as this could not have been written without the inspiration, encouragement, and cooperation of many ski instructors whose influence and experience helped shape the ideas expressed. To mention them all would be impossible. But it would be completely ungrateful to fail to express my deep appreciation to Joe Marillac, Joe Olivas and Henry Rist of the Parallel Ski School who first aroused my interest in ski teaching; to the Canadian Ski Instructors Alliance and Harvey Clifford who instilled the pride and stimulation of their professional approach to instructing; to Steve Eisner whose patience and special help in checking out the manuscript was invaluable; to Dave and Arthur Blumenthal, the photographers, who under adverse conditions and severe time limitations took all the superb photos that illustrate the book; to Art Parker, who generously made available the facilities at Thunder Mountain; to all my ski friends and relations whose keen interest kept the fires of enthusiasm burning; and lastly to Betty Slater, the co-author, who married me.

COLLIER QUICK AND EASY SERIES

SKIING WITH CONTROL

Chapter One

BEFORE YOU GO SKIING

Getting into Condition

THE MOST IMPORTANT single item of your skiing equipment is your body. It's the very first thing you should prepare for skiing. Chances are, as you read this, you aren't physically ready for the rigors ahead. For in skiing down snow-covered slopes your muscles will be subject to special stresses and strains. And for the average person, these muscles have a pretty soft time of it during a normal daily routine. Even if you are an energetic person who stays trim all year 'round, you'll find the muscles used in skiing are not the same as those used in most other activities.

There are at least four good reasons why you're urged to do this conditioning *before* you go skiing.

First, *you'll learn faster*. When your muscles are tight and you can't easily bend, stretch, or twist, it's pretty tough to learn any ski movements. If you're a neophyte this is even more applicable to you. The positions in which you will probably find yourself may be awkward and taxing. Your body must help, not hinder, your progress. It must respond when you call on it for action.

Second, *proper conditioning will minimize the amount of stiffness and aches* associated with the first days of skiing. Don't be a first-day ball of fire whose enthusiasm is extinguished by sore limbs. Good skiers precondition; they enjoy the early part of the season to the fullest. The season is short enough as it is. Why waste any of it?

Third, you greatly *reduce the chances of injury*

when you're in shape. This is true of all athletics, but particularly so in skiing. And here, the experienced skier has a distinct advantage. He is less vulnerable because he's not fighting unfamiliar sensations. He skis with ease instead of with effort. Because he has acquired skill he expends less energy, and so he needs less actual strength. Beginners have not yet reached that stage and should be in top shape.

Fourth, but not least, *you'll be missing plenty of fun if you can't keep up with your friends.*

Physical fitness experts find sagging muscles and flabby midrifts a national condition. With alarming regularity there are reports that detail the "disheartening trend toward physical deterioration among Americans." This is an era when most of us live easy but play hard. In the ski world, this is foolhardy.

So take a realistic look and see how physically fit you are. Be honest with yourself. The points to check are: your weight; the flexibility of your muscles; the strength of your muscles; your stamina or endurance. Let's take them one at a time.

A bathroom scale and a full-length mirror will quickly tell whether or not you have a weight problem. If you're a beginner or lower intermediate you'll bless the day you decided to trim down. In the early stages of learning you'll be climbing a fair amount of time. Hauling excess poundage up the slopes doesn't add any fun. Nor will extra flesh make it easier for you to pick yourself out of the snow. On the other hand, if you're excessively light, you'll find you tire easily and will have to quit early. If you have any question about the proper weight for your frame, consult your doctor.

Here are some tests which indicate how supple your muscles are.

1. Bend down and touch the floor in front of your toes. Keep your knees straight. Can you hold your fingers there for a slow count of 3?
2. Stand with your feet flat on the floor 5 or 6 inches apart. Sink into a deep knee-bend, keeping your heels on the floor, thrusting your arms forward. Are you able to get all the way down into a squatting position?
3. Stand with your back to a mirror. Keeping both feet together, twist around and look in the mirror. Can you see the front of both shoulders?
4. Stand facing a wall, about 3 inches from it, feet 5 or 6 inches apart. Keeping the upper body erect, push your hips down toward the floor so that your knees and ankles bend. Can you touch the wall with your knees?

Here are some yardsticks for judging the strength of your muscles.

1. Can you do a dozen deep knee-bends?
2. Can you do a half dozen sit-ups? (If you don't know or have forgotten how to do them, see p. 4.)
3. How many times can you push up from the floor? Did you raise your entire body properly or did you sag in the middle? (See p. 4 for instructions on doing push-ups.)
4. Stand with your back to a wall, about a foot in front of it, feet hip-width apart. Sink into a sitting position with your back and hips touching the wall, knees bent at right angles. Hold that position. Can the muscles in your upper leg take it for 20 seconds?
5. Can you run 100 yards at moderate speed without slowing down?
6. Can you bound up 2 flights of stairs rapidly, without feeling exahusted at the top?

Were you able to do all this easily? If so, you're in reasonably good starting shape. The rest of the way should not be difficult. If you didn't do so well with these "indication" checks, then you'd better begin your physical build-up right now.

A PROGRAM TO SPEED YOUR PHYSICAL BUILD-UP

Using Your Daily Routine
Walk whenever and wherever you can. Walk to and from work. If the distance makes that impossible,

walk part of the way. Park your car 6 or 8 blocks from your usual parking spot; or get off the bus 3 stops sooner and walk the rest. Give your legs a better workout every day. Although walking is a relatively mild form of exercise, it will help your overall conditioning.

Climb. Substitute leg exercise for elevators. This is more strenuous than walking, but also more beneficial. It builds leg strength in the calves, quads (the muscles just above the knee), and thighs. It also helps in the stamina department. If you work on the upper floor of a building, start by climbing the last flight. After a few days, get off the elevator 2 flights below and climb. Build up so that eventually you are walking up 4 flights daily. Use the stairs when you're shopping in department stores. Use them when visiting friends who don't live on the ground floor. Here's a tip that will multiply the benefits to your calves. When you go up the stairs, walk on your toes and the balls of your feet, instead of putting the entire foot down flat. Try it. See how quickly you feel the quad muscles working. Another tip: Walking down stairs is beneficial too. Use the same method of staying on your toes rather than on your entire foot.

Here's a habit you can incorporate easily into your daily living. It will help firm up your midsection, and no one will be able to detect the action. Pull in your abdomen and tighten your seat muscles as hard as you can. Hold it for a slow count of 10. Release. Repeat it. Good. You have just learned one of the little tricks many Hollywood stars use to keep their abdomens flat. You can practice the abdomen–seat-tightening routine frequently whenever you have 10 seconds to spare. You can do it while waiting for a traffic light to change, or for a bus—in fact you can even do it sitting down. The thing to remember is to practice it often—and always be sure to pull your muscles tight enough so they are under tension.

Proper diet is a cornerstone of good health. Eat good foods in moderate quantities. This aspect of preseason planning is so elementary, it's often overlooked. Eat fewer rich foods, creamy sauces, fattening desserts. How do you accomplish this without going on a crash diet? The best way is always to leave the table before you are completely satisfied. Eat a little bit less at each meal. Soon you will require less.

Exercising at Home
The second part of the program centers around exercises you can do at home. You won't need a lot

of equipment—just determination. You must do them regularly if they're to be of value. If you do these simple exercises faithfully, you're certain to see and feel results. The exercises suggested here are but a few of hundreds recommended by athletic coaches and ski pros. They were chosen to provide you with a balance of conditioning in the 3 main areas of your body which need conditioning: legs; mid-section; arms, back, and shoulders.

To Get Your Legs in Shape: Jump rope. Use a piece of ordinary laundry line or buy a child's jump rope. If you don't have either one, use an imaginary rope. Each day jump rope continuously for at least 50 jumps. Every 4 days add another 10 jumps until you're doing 100 every day. Stay on your toes and the balls of your feet when you push off and when you land. Use both feet—a habit you'll appreciate when you start to ski parallel. Trick: Make believe you're on a carton of fresh eggs. You don't want to break them. See how lightly you can take off and land. Let your ankles and knees absorb the landing. Here's a quick way to feel this gentleness. Keeping the upper body erect jump an inch or 2 off the ground. Try to land flat-footed. Notice how you jarred. Now jump again, but by contrast, land on the front part only. Allow your body to sink after your feet have made contact with the ground. Your knees and ankles act as shock absorbers. If you can get the feeling of this ankle action you'll be well on your way to a graceful style when you ski. Jumping rope will help you develop good spring action and at the same time it will strengthen the muscles in your calves and thighs.

Practice deep knee-bends. This is the skier's traditional exercise—and with good reason. It strengthens the upper leg muscles which are used in most modern ski movements. Do 12 to start and gradually increase until you are doing 25 in each workout. To further strengthen the upper leg muscles, try doing them on one leg. Do one or 2 as a starter and increase to 5 on each leg. If you can't maintain your balance, use a chair on each side to support your torso.

Use the knee-against-the-wall exercise to develop flexibility in your ankles and stretch your calves. Stand facing a wall. Bend your knees and ankles until your knees touch the wall. Move away from the wall until you're at the point where, by straining, your knees just touch it. Mark the place behind your heels. Each day assume this position and try to push your body lower so that you are stretching the calves and loosening the ankle and knee joints. When you

can touch the wall easily from that mark, move back a bit. The further away you can get and still touch, the better.

Do the raise-and-kick exercise to sharpen your sense of balance, while strengthening your ankles and calves. Stand with your arms at your sides. Raise yourself onto the ball of your left foot and kick the right one forward, waist high. At the same time raise your arms to shoulder level. Lower your arms and legs simultaneously. Repeat 12 times with each leg. As you get the feel of this exercise raise your leg higher. You should feel the thigh muscles stretching.

Work on the side-to-side jump. Draw 2 parallel lines on the floor about a foot apart. If you're on a carpeted surface, use 2 pieces of string. Pretend the area between the lines is freshly painted. You want to jump over, without getting your feet wet. Stand to the left of the "paint." Jump from one side of the line and back again to the other in a continuous series of jumps, pressing your feet together and keeping your upper body erect. Don't pause between jumps. Make the landing of one jump the springboard for the next. This will help teach you to use your legs together as a unit and to balance the upper body over them. (If you are an experienced skier, try jumping from the left traverse position to the right traverse position, back to the left, etc.) Points to keep in mind: see how lightly you can land; use both feet at the same time; keep the upper body movement to a minimum. Start by doing a group of 4 consecutive jumps, repeated 6 times. Gradually increase so that you can do 6 or 8 jumps in each series.

The skiers' invisible throne is another exercise that will strengthen your quad and thigh muscles. Sit in an imaginary throne, back flat against a wall with your knees out at right angles, your feet directly underneath them. Keep your arms and hands flat against the wall. Hold this position as long as your muscles will support you. Carefully time yourself. For the next 3 days, "sit" for the same length of time. Then start to increase the time each day until you can remain in that position for 60 seconds. *This is one of the most important exercises you can do.* When you ski, most of the time you will be relying on these same quad and thigh muscles.

To Get Your Mid-Section in Shape: Practice the roll-over leg touch. Lie flat on your back, arms extended. Roll your right leg over and touch your outstretched left hand, keeping your left leg stationary. Roll back in the opposite direction and kick your left leg up to your right hand. Repeat until you have kicked each leg across 12 times.

Now try sit-ups. Lie flat on your back, hands behind your neck, feet wedged under a chair or piece of furniture. (Or have someone kneel and hold them.) Raise your entire torso. Sit up, come forward, and touch your left elbow to your right knee. Lower yourself slowly to the floor. Sit up and touch the right elbow to the left knee. Repeat 6 times with each elbow touch. Gradually increase until you are doing 12 with each.

Another effective exercise is the over-the-head touch. Lie on your back, arms at your sides, palms down. Keeping your legs straight, raise them over your head until they touch the floor behind. Then lower them slowly until they are 2 inches off the ground. Hold them there. Count to 10. Raise your legs over your head and again touch the floor behind. Lower them ever so slowly and hold them just off the floor. Repeat this 5 times to start. Increase until you are doing the exercise 10 times before bringing your feet to rest on the floor.

The side tilt will also help condition your midriff. Stand with your feet comfortably apart, with the palms of your hands touching the sides of your legs. Keeping your hands against your body, slide your left hand down your left leg as far as you can. Return to your original position. Reach down on the right side as far as you can. Reach 12 times on each side.

TO BUILD STRENGTH IN YOUR ARMS, SHOULDERS AND BACK: Do push-ups, another favorite exercise of athletic instructors everywhere. It works. Lie on your stomach with your hands at your chest and pointing forward, elbows bent. Push up from the floor, keeping your entire body straight, until your elbows snap into an upright position. Men should start with 6 push-ups and increase by one each day until they are doing 15. Girls can start with one and do one more each day until they can do 3.

Between each set of exercises do this relaxer. Hang over from the waist and go limp. Let your arms hang. Then bounce the trunk toward the floor, as if you were a marionette whose strings were just cut. Next, stand up again and shake out each leg a dozen times. Try to flop the foot as if you were slowly shaking off water. This will take less than a minute, and will clear away tensions so that you're ready for the next exercise.

Exercising with Groups of People

Because it's more fun to do your conditioning with a group of people, check with your local YMCA or YWCA, schools, and ski clubs. Most probably there is a nearby group that has a preseason training program. Join it. You'll find that conditioning is much more fun, competitive, and profitable when you are part of a group activity.

Exercising with Your Ski Equipment

The last part of the overall program consists of exercises using your ski equipment. If you haven't acquired skis and boots yet, now is the time to get them. First, wear your boots around the house. It takes time for your feet to get used to ski boots. You might just as well do it before the season. Five or six active hours spread over 2 or 3 days should serve the purpose. After your feet become accustomed to the boots, you're ready to start working with both the boots and the skis.

Now put on your skis and walk around your back yard or any other grassy place. First walk in big circles. Then side-step. That is, step the right ski to the right, and bring the left one over to it. Step, together, step, together in this fashion 15 or 20 yards to the right. Then side-step back to your original spot, left ski to the left, bringing the right ski to it. Next walk in a pattern of large figure 8's.

Another exercise to do with your skis and boots on your feet: lift your left leg and ski out to the side. At the same time, bend your right knee and ankle as you balance on the right leg. Return to your original position. Swing your left leg 6 times. Then repeat the exercise, balancing on the left leg and lifting the right. As you lift, push the knee of the balancing leg as far forward as you can. If you can't bend the ankle try loosening your boots at the instep.

The idea is simple. Get accustomed to the weight of the skis now, and you'll learn much faster when you get out on the snow.

Summary: Many people get everything in shape for skiing but themselves. This just doesn't make much sense. Be physically fit and you'll have more fun. You'll learn quicker. You'll have fewer aches and stiff joints, and you won't be left behind by your friends. You don't have to be a Charles Atlas to enjoy skiing. Just be sure the muscles you have are ready.

The authors consider physical conditioning so important to your ability to learn, that they urge you to plan your own individual program even before you read further in this book. If your daily routine doesn't allow you to do all of the exercises, don't abandon the entire program. Pick one for the legs, one for the mid-section, one for the arms. A 10-

minute workout every morning or evening is better than no program.

MENTAL PREPARATIONS

Your attitude toward skiing has a great deal to do with how rapidly you learn and how much fun you have while doing it. You should realize that it takes a certain number of hours (the number varies from person to person, naturally), just to get to the point where the skis no longer feel like rowboats on your feet. The sooner you put on your skis and start to walk around, the sooner you arrive at the point where you can manage the skis easily.

The same principle applies to each maneuver. You may have to make 100 practice stem christies before you get the smooth rhythmic feeling of it. If you make only 10 turns a day it will take 10 days before you get it. If you practice making 25 turns in the morning and another 25 in the afternoon, you'll learn it in one weekend.

Follow the plan of the book, learning each maneuver in the sequence in which it appears. Don't skip to the advanced section (parallel skiing) without having practiced the movements and exercises that lead up to it. You'll be wasting your time and will probably unjustly degrade your coordination and ability if you fail to do the advanced maneuvers properly. On the other hand, if you read and understand why you're learning each new maneuver, you'll see how this plan will build your ability to control the skis, surely and safely. Just recognize the fact that it takes time to overcome many of the natural instincts which must be discarded if you're going to be a skier. For instance, you'll be tempted to lean into the hill at the very time when you should be leaning away from the hill. Leaning out is something that has to be learned. You don't do it instinctively. As long as you're progressing within the plan, be satisfied. Don't expect to ski like your instructor the first weekend out.

Falling is part of learning. This is a realistic fact, so don't be embarrassed if you do. Of course, you're encouraged to avoid as many falls as you possibly can. But you will fall, just like everyone else who ever learned how to ski. The principles of safe falling explained on page 42 are worthy of careful study.

Some instructors figure that confidence is about 70 per cent of your ability to learn and have fun. We think it rates even higher. How do you acquire confidence? There are four general rules.

1. Practice each maneuver until you have become reasonably adept at it before tackling the next one.

2. Ski on slopes that are safe for the level of your ability. From time to time, you may have to ski on slopes a little more difficult than those you're accustomed to, but be sure they are only a *little* steeper, or narrower. Don't be led astray by friends who are eager to take you down the expert trails when you aren't ready for them.

3. Start out each new day on skis by skiing slopes you know you can handle. After you get the feel of the skis and the snow, begin to practice the next more advanced exercise or movement. Trying to get down a slope that's too much for you first thing in the morning can ruin your entire day!

4. Finally, add the important ingredient, *relaxation,* to your skiing.

Choosing Your Equipment

Good equipment is a must for anyone who intends to learn how to ski properly. The word "good" refers to equipment that is adequate for your individual needs and intentions, and not necessarily expensive. Whether you intend to ski two or twenty-two days during the season, your equipment will be a major factor in determining how quickly you learn. As soon as you have learned to walk and climb, you'll be starting to ski downhill. You'll be learning to control your skis. For this, boots, skis, bindings, and poles specifically suited to your height, weight, and athletic ability are essential.

Your enjoyment of the sport is directly related to your ability to control the skis. Good equipment not only adds to your fun, but definitely reduces the chance of injury. How should you go about getting it? *Go to a reputable ski shop where you can discuss your individual situation with people experienced in helping skiers such as yourself.*

You will be able to rent equipment (if you want to delay making an investment until you've tried skiing a few times), or you can buy it. Whatever you choose to do, resist the temptation to use your friends' cast-off skis or boots if they aren't right for your size and weight. (Specific ways to test this are described on the following pages.) No matter how good their intentions may be, your friends will be doing you a distinct disservice if they persuade you to use skis and boots that are the wrong size for you.

When you decide to buy, you will have a vast selection of equipment. The wonderful part is that you have so many choices in each price range. In that respect, you are a lot more fortunate than the skiers who began before you. Constant research and testing have enabled manufacturers to develop improvements that make lower- and moderate-priced equipment more effective than anything previously available, regardless of price. With each new ski season, so many new models and new products are put on the market that it has become impossible for the average pleasure skier to keep up with them. That's why you should buy your equipment in a well-stocked, reliable ski shop, where you'll get really competent advice.

Buying ski equipment, particularly boots, does take time. Allow yourself ample time to browse, try on several kinds, discuss the relative merits of each, and think about your intended purchases. Don't put yourself into a position where you'll be rushed into buying. A good idea is to try to shop at an off hour when the ski shop won't be crowded, and the sales people can spend a maximum amount of time with you. Above all, don't buy anything that isn't what you want. Remember, you'll be using the ski equipment for a long time. Make sure it's adequate for your needs. Shop during the early part of the season, before the stocks become depleted.

Here is a rundown, item by item, of what to look for when buying ski equipment. It will acquaint you with the various things you'll need and will also give you an idea of the important considerations when buying.

SKI BOOTS

Ski boots are listed first because they are the most important item you will buy. They transmit your body movements to your skis and are thus critical to your control. If they are too loose, your leg action will be dissipated inside your boots. This is like having a loose connection between your steering wheel and the wheels themselves; you turn the wheel but there isn't any reaction where it counts. If your boots are too tight, you'll quickly develop painful blisters and tender spots. *The fit of your boots is the prime consideration.*

Ski boots must be snug, particularly in the heel. Yet they must be comfortable. You'll be wearing them anywhere from five to eight hours during the course of a ski day. Be sure your toes are not cramped. You should be able to wiggle them and thus keep circulation.

Here are the desirable characteristics to seek. First, look for a double boot construction. This in effect is a boot within a boot. The inner boot holds your foot firmly, while the outer one provides the solid support. You need strong lateral support so that the sideways movement of your feet is immediately imparted to your skis. At the same time, you need front-back suppleness so you can bend your ankles forward. Many boots have special hinged backs and other construction features designed for this very

Ski boots—highlighting various features.

purpose. Look for inside padding, usually foam rubber, around the top and the ankle, along the length of the tongue, and vertically on each side of the heel, to give you added comfort. (This is not essential, but certainly desirable.) Many boots have back laces, ankle straps, or other tightening devices to insure a snug heel fit. Some are more practical than others. Ask at the ski shop for the relative merits of each. Boots must also keep out the cold and moisture. Look at the workmanship around the welt, where the sole is sewn to the uppers. Hand-stitching here usually is a plus. The best boots are triple-stitched, another plus, but not an essential. Look at the bottom of the boot. It should have some type of non-skid rubber sole, securely attached to the main leather sole. Several manufacturers have recently marketed boots which use buckle closings in place of laces. This feature is a real convenience but is not more important than proper fit.

Here is a good way to try on boots. Put on one of your own woolen athletic socks (bring a pair with you). Slip your foot into the boot slowly, without letting your sock bunch up. Kick your heel down on the floor, setting your foot against the back of the boot. Lace the boot up (the inner boot if there is one) with your foot in that same position—heel against the floor, toes pointed upward. Since the inner boot is not the prime source of support, it should not be too tight. Lace up the outer laces with more firmness. Now stand up and walk a few steps to get a general feel of the fit. Can you wiggle your toes easily? You should be able to.

Squat on your haunches, then reach down and hold the heel of the boot at the sole to the floor.

Girls not wearing slacks should ask someone to hold the heel of the boot. Lift the heel of your foot. The boot should come with it without any delay. For comparison, hold the back of your other shoe. Lift the heel of that foot. Notice how far your heel moves before the shoe starts to come with it. A good test for adequate toe room is to unlace the boot, and push your foot forward until it touches the front of the boot. There should now be just enough room behind your heel to slide your index finger into the back of the boot.

Try on both boots. Many people are not aware that one foot may differ slightly in size and shape from the other. It will be well worth your time to make certain both boots fit your feet properly. As a final check put the boots on a flat surface, such as the glass counter top, and see whether the soles are flat. They should be free of any curling.

Here are some other suggestions which should be helpful to you when buying boots:

1. Disregard the sizes marked on the box and inside the boot itself. Ski-boot sizes differ from standard shoe sizes, and each manufacturer has his own lasts which vary in contour. The only thing that counts is how the boots feel on you.

2. Don't be bashful about trying on boots of different makers. After you have tried on several, you will have a much better basis for judging the difference between a snug fit and an improper fit.

3. Leather does stretch, since it is constantly exposed to moisture, and softens as a result. It is better to buy boots a trifle too snug than too loose.

4. If you know from experience in buying street shoes that you have unusually difficult feet to fit, consider having boots custom-made to your feet. They will cost more, but they may be worth it to you.

5. If you decide to buy buckle boots, be sure you have a good fit without the buckles being in the extreme positions. In this way, you'll be able to make further adjustments in the fit when your feet swell or if the leather softens.

6. Buy the very best boot you can afford. Forego some of the after-ski items if you have a budget problem, but invest in well-made, properly fitting boots. If you buy quality the first time, you will have good boots that will last you several seasons.

SKIS

Most ski shops stock a great variety of skis in all price brackets. You shouldn't have any difficulty in buying a pair suited to your height, weight, ski experience, and budget. Here are some guide posts to use when shopping for skis.

The length of the skis is correlated to your height. Stand with your arm raised straight up in the air. Hold the ski with the tail on the floor. If the ski is normal length for you the tip should come up to the heel of your hand. Slightly shorter skis will be somewhat easier for you to maneuver, if you are a beginner. But the shorter the skis, the less stability they will have. If you buy skis that are too long for you, you will have unnecessary difficulty in turning and maneuvering them. Normal length skis are recommended unless you've had no previous athletic experience, or you are just starting to ski and are beyond middle age. Then, a size or two shorter than normal will probably suit you better.

The flexibility of the skis you choose depends on your weight and your skiing ability. Soft or flexible skis turn easily and perform well in powder (light, dry unpacked snow); but they do not track (hold a straight course) or hold as well on very hard packed snow or in icy conditions as stiffer skis do. Stiff skis will be more stable at high speeds. They tend to hold better on ice, but it takes much greater turning effort and skill to turn them. Between the two extremes you'll find the majority of skis, designated as "standard" flex, or "all-round," or "combi." Unless you plan to own more than one pair, medium flexibility is your best bet. Since the designations differ from manufacturer to manufacturer, don't rely solely on the markings. Test the skis yourself and feel the flexibility of each.

There are two easy tests you can use. First, hold the skis upright, bottom-to-bottom, with the tails on the floor. Grasp the skis in the middle (approximately where your feet will be) and squeeze them. You should be able to press them together so that they touch evenly up and down the entire running surface. Men should be able to do this with one hand. The second test for flexibility is to take one ski and brace the tail against your shoe or against the wall. Hold the ski, running surface down, with one hand near the tip. With your other hand, press down on the ski sharply and let it spring back. After you have flexed several skis, you will be able to feel the difference in flexibility. If your weight is above average, you will probably do best with a slightly stiffer ski. If you are on the light side, a slightly softer pair will help you.

The camber of the skis is the upward curve in the middle of the skis and is correlated to your weight. It's built into the skis so that when the skier stands on them his weight will be distributed over the length of the running surface. Your weight should be sufficient to flatten out the skis when they are placed on the floor. If you aren't heavy enough to flatten a particular pair, you will have trouble turning them because your weight will be concentrated in the front and back of the skis. Conversely, if there isn't sufficient camber, your weight will be concentrated in the middle of the skis, making it easier for you to turn but depriving you of the steadiness you should be getting. If you can't find the perfect pair, it's better to select a pair with a bit less camber than with a bit too much.

There are five groups of materials from which skis are made: solid wood, laminated wood (many layers of woods pressed, glued, and molded together), various metals, fiberglass, and plastic. In solid wooden skis, hickory and other hard woods are the most desirable. They will give the best performance and are more durable than the soft woods. Laminated wooden skis are usually more expensive but generally are more durable and have more life, depending upon the skill of the individual manufacturer. Metal skis are known to be easy-turning skis, well suited to powder snow skiing, but may not be as stable on hard pack. They have a long life and require practically no care whatever; but are more expensive. Once again, these are merely generalities. Each manufacturer has built different characteristics into his skis. As for the fiberglas, epoxy, and other plastic skis, they vary so widely that each model must be judged separately. Your ski shop can advise

Running surfaces should provide durable protection against moisture. They should be smooth enough to slide easily on snow. Nowadays, most skis are made with either sheet plastic or sprayed plastic

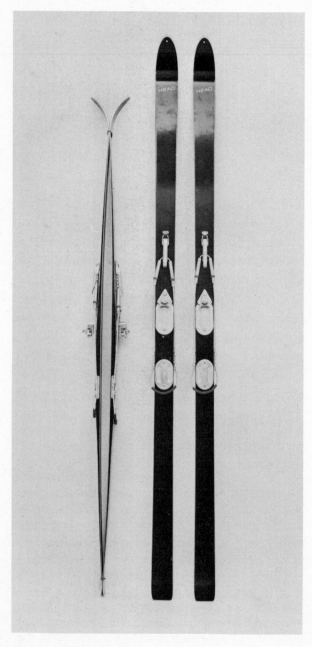

Skis. Side view shows camber.

bottoms. Some of these are harder and more resistant to gouging and scratching. Ask your ski shop salesman for the relative merits of the different types.

Most skis made today have metal edges along the length of the running surface, so that you can prevent the skis from slipping sideways when you want to and can get a bite, or hold, in the snow. Many have "offset edges" that jut out beyond the width of the ski itself. Although they are sometimes difficult for beginners to handle at first, they are a distinct advantage once you have had some edging experience and are beyond the exercise in edge control. Run your index finger along the bottom surface of the edges, from the tip down to the tail of the ski. It should be one smooth surface, free from any protrusions, such as screw heads or poorly joined pieces of edge.

Pleasure skis have a single groove down the middle of the running surface. This gives the skis their tracking qualities (ability to stay on a straight course until you turn them). Several manufacturers have brought out multi-grooved bottoms, but these have not proven to be superior.

You want skis that are free from any warping or twisting, otherwise they will probably not track, nor will they turn with equal facility to each direction. To test for warping lay one ski at a time flat on a level surface and try to rock it sideways from the tail of the ski. There should be no movement and it should remain flat until you tilt the entire ski. Another test is to rest the tip of the ski on a chair or shelf, running surface upward. Then put the other ski directly on it, running surface down. Holding the tails of both skis, look into the space between the skis from the tails toward the tips. Look at any part of the running surface, from side to side; the distance between the skis should be even. You should not be able to get any sideways rocking movement when you try to rock the tails.

Competition skis are becoming more popular among the expert pleasure skiers, although they are not built to last a lifetime of pleasure skiing. They do have special characteristics constructed into their design. Slalom skis are generally narrower with stiffer tips to give the competitor instant response to his turning action. Partially covered edges make the running surface slightly faster. The offset edges provide a good edge bite but they are not suited to soft snow skiing. Downhill skis are designed to be steady at high speeds. They are usually stiffer, beefier, and longer than the skis the same competitor would use for pleasure skiing. Most pleasure skiers find it difficult to turn downhill skis, particularly at slower

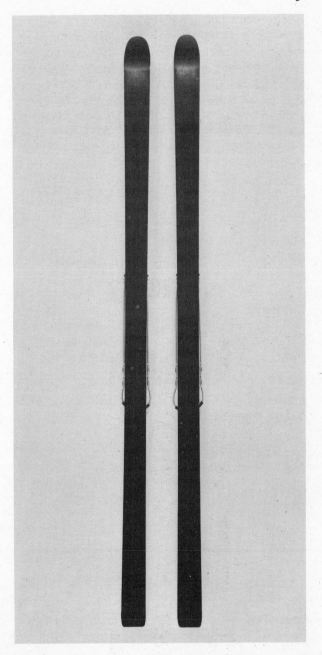

Skis with metal edges.

speeds. Giant slalom skis have characteristics that fall some place between the other two, since the giant slalom competition itself is almost a combination of slalom and downhill. According to an examination of slow motion movies of recent competitions, movements of competitors skiing giant slalom have the closest relationship to the movements of recreational skiers. Nevertheless, giant slalom skis are not recommended for beginners or intermediate skiers. Competition skis are expensive, and this is one time when the expensive item would be a bad choice for the beginner.

There are many fine well-known skis imported from Europe, and more recently some from Japan. They are usually measured in the metric system. This table comparing standard sizes shows the equivalent sizes in feet and inches:

EUROPEAN MEASUREMENTS	AMERICAN AND CANADIAN EQUIVALENTS	
Centimeters	Feet	Inches
220	7	3
215	7	1
210	6	11
205	6	9
200	6	7
195	6	5
190	6	3
185	6	1
180	5	11

BINDINGS

Bindings are the hardware which holds your boots to the skis. In recent years, manufacturers have developed special bindings which, under excess stress or tension of a fall, will free your boots from their fixed position on the skis. We strongly recommend that you buy one of the many release bindings available. There are more than four dozen makes and models on the market to choose from. The largest group of bindings consists of a toe unit, against which the boots are held firm. A cable runs around the back of the boot holding down the heel and a front throw mechanism controls the tension on the cable. Although manufacturers market the complete toe unit and front throw cable, you can purchase the toe unit separately and use it with the front throw cable from another make or model. In this way you can combine the advantages of many different models. Another group are called "boot-locks," which consist of a toe unit and a heel unit sold together as a complete binding. There is a pressure point at the toe and the heel. Either will release under tension. For advanced skiers, there is a turntable unit which allows the boot to swivel from its fixed position. This unit is used with a long leather strap called a "long thong," which wraps many times around the foot and ankle —not recommended for beginners or intermediates.

Different bindings will release your boots when

Bindings—release action.

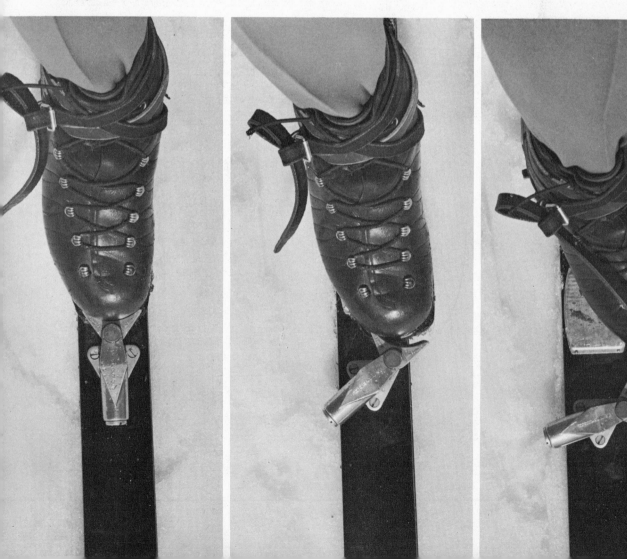

put under excess tension from different directions. Most release laterally (when the tension is from a fall to the side). Some release forward, some when you fall forward or backward. Many release if there is a twisting action. Still others release from more than one angle. Ask the ski shop people to demonstrate how each one releases and from which angles. Next, ask them to show you how the release mechanism is adjusted. You will then have a basis for comparing the construction and ease of operation and deciding.

A release binding is effective only if it is properly adjusted to your weight and ability. If it is set to release under too little stress, it will cause unnecessary spills and be a nuisance. If set too tight, it won't release when you need it to—which is as bad as not having a release binding at all.

A good idea is to let the ski shop where you buy the bindings mount them on your skis. They will be thoroughly familiar with the bindings and will be experienced in mounting and adjusting them to your weight and ability. Another reason for having a reliable shop do the mounting is that the position of the bindings on the skis is very important to the action of the skis. However, it will be up to you to check your release adjustments each time you put on your skis. Often the settings will change without your knowing it, and they sometimes become clogged with frozen snow and ice. *Test them before you put on your skis, each and every time.*

Consider buying an Arlberg strap. This is a leather strap which attaches to the cable and wraps around the ankle. In addition, it prevents the ski from running away if the binding releases. Runaway skis can injure somebody below you on the hill. Many ski areas do not permit skiers to wear release bindings unless they are also wearing a leash, an Arlberg strap, or some other safety device.

POLES

Your poles are an important part of your equipment. When skiing, you will use them constantly. You will carry them for balance, lean on them for support, push with them, and pivot around them. They make it easier for you to maneuver and move in all directions. We therefore suggest that you get the lightest ski poles you can in your proper length. You will handle them with maximum dexterity. Lightweight poles are especially important to girls, who do not have the arm muscle development most men do.

The weight of the poles is largely dependent upon the material used in the shaft. Four materials are most commonly used. Tonkin bamboo poles are very light and inexpensive, but not as durable as the metal or fiberglass poles. They are recommended for all girls, and except for a huge heavy-set man (in which case they may not be sturdy enough), they are probably the best all-around choice for men, too. Aluminum tubing is also lightweight but more durable than bamboo. The best aluminum poles have been treated to resist cutting, which weakens the poles and causes snap-off. They are more expensive than bamboo. Steel tubing is probably the sturdiest material used, but heavy. Poles of this material are not as expensive as the hard coated aluminum. Fiberglass is lightweight, but it tends to be too resilient.

The length of the pole relates directly to your height. Here is a simple way to find the proper length. Hold the poles with the points resting on the floor. The tops of the handles should come up to your armpits. Actually, when you are skiing, the effective length of the poles will be a bit shorter, as the points are pushed into the snow up to the baskets. The length not only affects the weight of your poles, but even more important, it affects your body position when skiing. If you choose poles that are too short, you will have to bend forward (improperly) from the waist to put them into the snow. And when you climb, they won't give you support unless you bend out of position. If your poles are too long, they will cause you to carry your arms too high, which often leads to sitting back on the skis.

The feel of the poles is something you must experience with each different make. Slip your hand up through the leather strap handle, then bring your palm forward, grasping the handle and the two straps between your thumb and forefinger. Raise the tip of the pole until it is horizontal. Wave the tip up and down, then sideways a few times. You will feel the weight and the balance of the pole. Compare a few different makes and you'll quickly feel their individual differences.

The rings or baskets should be lightweight but durable. Carefully examine the way in which they are fastened to the shaft. This is the area of your ski poles that bears the brunt of the pressure when you thrust with them. Hint: Most baskets are connected with a leather piece and a cotter pin through the shaft. The cotter pin is usually below the ring. Usually this is the part of the pole which wears out first. By unfastening the ring and re-attaching it with the leather piece inverted and the ring below the cotter pin, you can strengthen your ski pole. The ring itself, instead of the less sturdy leather piece and cotter pin, will come in contact with the snow. Also, you are adding effective length to your pole

a) Poles.

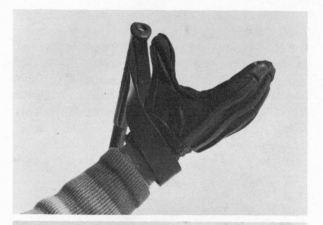

b) Getting into poles.

as you make the distance from the tip to the basket smaller. This means that you can buy a pole an inch or two shorter, move the baskets to the lower position of the shaft, and end up with the proper length of pole which is even lighter than your normal selection.

The handles or grips should be comfortable for your hand (a matter of personal preference) and they should have straps long enough for you to get in and out easily when you're wearing ski mittens or gloves. Leather grips are usually sewn together.

Since the stitching is repeatedly exposed to hard use and wet snow, it often comes undone. Plastic or hard rubber grips are constructed in one piece and are trouble-free. Some handles have contour finger grips, a plus feature, but not essential.

Recently there have been poles on the market which feature release grips. Under severe pressure, the handles of the poles will separate from the shafts. Since we have not had any experience with these poles, we suggest you ask the ski shop for their experience and opinions of them.

BOOT PRESSES

The boot press is a device which keeps the soles of your boots flat when you aren't wearing them. Curling of the soles will cause problems with the way your boots fit into the bindings. The boot press will make it easy for you to carry your boots, store them during the off season, and keep the leather in shape. Your ski shop will probably have a few different kinds to choose from. Boot presses are inexpensive items, but most worthwhile.

SOLVING THE CLOTHING PROBLEM

When you go out skiing, you must be warm; your outer garments must be *water-resistant* as well as windproof; and you must have freedom of movement (particularly in the arms and shoulders, legs, and seat). These are the basic requirements for your clothing. Style and high fashion have been introduced comparatively recently to ski wear, and you'll see many beautiful articles of ski clothing when you shop. We encourage you to be as well dressed as you can. It will help your morale. But don't sacrifice functional qualities for appearance when you are getting together your ski outfit.

Some general rules regarding your ski clothing may be helpful to your overall planning.

1. Many skiers have found it advantageous for the first weekend or two to ski in clothing they already owned or could borrow. Then, with this experience behind them, they were able to shop with a much clearer idea of their needs.

2. To feel warm when you are outside in below freezing weather, your extremities must be warm. Toes, fingertips, and ears are susceptible to the cold, so don't gloss over the importance of your socks, mittens, and hat.

3. You will be warmer wearing several layers of lighter clothing than with one heavier layer.

4. Darker colors are more practical for beginning skiers. They don't smudge, stain, or discolor so easily. Light-colored pants and parkas can be dry-cleaned, but they usually lose their water repellent qualities in the process.

5. Be sure you have at least three or four pockets. You will want to carry money, handkerchiefs or tissues, lip ice, cigarettes, a candy bar, wax, and so on, in an easy-to-get-at-pocket.

Socks

Most people find that the best way to keep their feet warm is to wear two pairs of socks; a thin lightweight pair next to their feet and woolen athletic socks over them. Be sure they fit smoothly. Bunched or wrinkled socks will raise blisters as quickly as they will lower your enthusiasm. Socks that are too tight will cramp your feet. Wear your socks inside your pants. If you wear them on the outside, they will collect snow, which sticks to wool. In a short while, the melted snow will run through your socks.

Underwear

During the winter part of the ski season, warm underwear is an essential first layer. The fit is important. The proper size should allow you complete ease of movement. Underwear that's too small will pull and constrict your motion. In addition to the discomfort, it will hinder your ability to learn. Underwear that's too big will bunch up—also a source of annoyance.

Two-piece underwear gives you greater flexibility than the one-piece kind. When spring comes, you will probably want to dispense with your winter weight top, but you may want to continue to wear the bottom.

Thermal underwear, originally developed for arctic and mountain climbing expeditions, has been a boon to skiers. It affords maximum warmth. There are several types available: waffle weave, fish net, and a special construction of cotton and wool. All embody the same principle of trapping your body heat in the tiny air spaces between the layers of fabric. If you wear one of the fish net types, wear a closely woven garment immediately over it to keep the body heat in.

All-wool ski underwear also provides the needed warmth, in some cases with less bulk than thermal underwear. We are partial to the combination of all-wool bottoms and thermal tops.

Ski Pants

Your ski pants should be water-repellent and should give you enough room to bend, squat, and stretch without restriction. Warmth is not really a factor. Your underwear will provide that. Closely-woven, smooth fabrics (such as gabardine) are water-repellent and windproof. Stretch pants, made from elasticized fabrics in a rainbow of colors, are styled for a trim, glamorous appearance. They are expensive and not essential for the beginning skier. If you can afford them, they are the best. But invest first in good equipment, then in stylish clothing.

When choosing ski pants, carefully check the piece that goes under your foot to hold the pants down in the boots. Narrow elastic bands tend to cut into the bottom of the feet. A wide band of material or elastic is more satisfactory. Look at the manner in which the under-foot band is secured. This is the part of the pants which wears first.

Well-made ski pants usually have a band of elastic and rubber around the waist. This prevents tucked-in shirts or sweaters from riding up. If your ski pants don't have it, you can buy a yard of this special banding and have it sewn in. Try on the ski pants before you buy them. Don't rely on the waist size or any other marked measurement. Each brand of ski pants is cut with a different line. The size in one brand that fits you best may not be the same size in another. Look for pockets that are deep enough to hold the things you'll be carrying.

Sweaters

The very last items you ought to spend your money on are sweaters. Almost any kind you already own will do. And the principle of two light layers giving more warmth and comfort than one heavy bulky layer holds true for sweaters. One satisfactory way to get more body warmth without bulking up the arms is to wear a sleeveless sweater underneath one with sleeves.

Although pullovers seem to be most popular, cardigans have the advantage of allowing you to wear them with the fronts open. When you come into the warming hut, you can leave your cardigan on and simply unbutton it. And girls can get them on and off without mussing their hair. Woolen, flannel, or corduroy shirts make good substitutes for sweaters.

Parkas

To be effective, your parka must be windproof, water-resistant, and roomy enough to allow you to swing your arms and shoulders freely. The most practical for beginning skiers is the shell type. These are made of unlined nylon, Byrd cloth, Zelan, or specially treated poplin. Shells can be worn during the winter and spring season. With these parkas, which are not worn for warmth, you can adjust the layers underneath to suit the varying degrees of cold. Often parkas of this type are reversible, a fashion bonus for you.

Quilted parkas are becoming more and more popular. They are much warmer than the shell type. They are also generally bulkier, and certainly more expensive, and are usually too warm for spring skiing.

Many parkas have hoods which fold up into the collars. This is really a useful extra, which you'll be glad you have when you ski during a heavy snow storm. Styles that zip up the front are easier to get into and out of than pullovers.

Color is naturally a matter of personal taste. But some of the high-fashion light colors are not practical, especially for beginners. They soil too easily, and dry cleaning will take out much, if not all, of their water repellency.

Adequate pockets, deep enough to hold your goggles or hat, are an advantage. Waterproof golf jackets or military jackets have proven satisfactory for a number of neophyte skiers.

Gloves or Mittens

There is hardly anything more discouraging to your desire to ski than cold fingers. Mittens are definitely warmer than gloves. And although gloves afford a better feel and more control of the ski poles, in the early stages of learning the warmth of mittens is more important. In either case, look for reinforced palms, which will stand up better under the friction of rope tow riding. Also, whether you buy mittens or gloves, outer shells plus separate liners are invariably warmer than the one-piece lined types. The liners should be wool. The gauntlet or long style which pulls over your parka sleeve will keep the snow out if it is not loose fitting. You can add your own snap or button to the gauntlet to keep it closed.

If you decide to buy gloves, be sure there is enough room at your finger tips. Tight gloves constrict circulation and will be painfully cold. Then examine the stitching of the fingers. The longest wearing gloves are those *without* seams or stitching on the palm side of the individual fingers. Seams that are exposed to wear against the pole grip will open sooner or later. You can repair outside stitching yourself. Inside stitching usually has to be resewn by a cobbler or tailor.

Hats

Almost anything goes in the way of head-gear. The only consideration is to keep your head, and particularly your ears, warm.

Goggles

A good pair of goggles will protect your eyes from wind, snow, and the bright glare of sun reflecting off snow. They are a must, not optional equipment. You'll quickly find out that when you can't see very well, you won't be able to ski very well either. Try to buy goggles that have changeable lenses to meet the various light and weather conditions: brown or green for sunny days; amber or yellow to highlight contours on dull days; clear for average or windy days.

Many have air holes cut into the sides and top to prevent fogging. These are only partly successful.

The best way to get a pair of fog-proof goggles is to make them yourself by taping a second lens onto the outside of the regular lens. The seal must be airtight. Then the two lenses will act the same way as the double windows of airplanes work—on the air insulation principle.

Chapter Two

WHAT PLEASURE SKIING IS ALL ABOUT

THE ESSENCE OF pleasure skiing is turning gracefully and with precise control.

One way or another, good skiers are always in motion, always turning. They turn to set up rhythm. They turn to control their speed. They make quick, sharp turns to negotiate steep or narrow places. They make wide, sweeping turns to come down open slopes. They even turn sharply back uphill to come to a complete stop.

Obviously, not all these turns are the same. There are literally dozens of different turns and variations used by pleasure skiers. The skill you develop in learning to execute the various kinds of turns will govern the amount of control you achieve and the smoothness of your style.

What is it that will make your skis turn? It isn't one factor alone, but a combination of factors: *turning power, unweighting, and edge control*. Since the skis won't turn of their own accord, you must generate the turning force; either by moving parts of your body in a rotary fashion, or by shifting your weight from one ski to the other. In most turns, you'll use both sources of turning power. Then to make it easier for your skis to turn, you reduce the friction between the skis and the snow. You take the weight off your legs and skis (called "unweighting") either by raising the body ("lift") or by rapidly dropping the hips ("drop"). Although both methods are effective, skiing with the lift is more practical at slow and moderate speeds, and skiing with drop is more practical at high speeds. The third factor, edge control, is more subtle than the other two and usually takes longest to master. So that your body movements take effect on the snow, you must learn to control your edges (angle them into the snow to get more "bite," flatten them to run smoothly, or change from edging one side of the ski to edging the other side). Edge control is achieved by pressing the knees and ankles into or away from the hill while the rest of the body counterbalances.

When you're not in the process of turning, you'll probably be traversing. This is the position you'll use when skiing down the hill diagonally. As a pleasure skier, you won't be spending a great deal of time skiing directly down the hill as you would if you were training to become a racer. Nine-tenths of the time you'll be traversing or turning.

In modern skiing, emphasis is on economy of motion. The thinking behind this is simple. The less body movement needed to produce the action you want, the quicker you can do it and the easier it will be for you to stay balanced. This philosophy originated among the international ski teams. Competitors could not afford a single bit of unnecessary expenditure of motion or energy—not if they wanted to win. So they devised methods of controlling the skis that required a minimum of body movement but yielded a maximum of control. Ski schools followed these developments closely; analyzing films and photos of competitions, and listening to what these elite skiers had to say. They then adapted these techniques and principles to pleasure skiing.

The most important of these principles is this: Although you use your entire body when skiing, it is *the lower half that does most of the work*. Modern skiing is "leg action" skiing. You generate turning power from your legs. You absorb the unevenness of the slope in your legs. Your basic edge control comes from ankle, knee, and hip action. The upper body which remains relatively upright has been rele-

a) Ankle and knee bend.

b) Knee and waist bend.

gated to a minor role, providing the grace and balance to the movements taking place below the waist. These upper body movements are minimal by comparison to the leg action.

The concept of skiing like a playful panther is worth mentioning here. It refers to the use of the ankle joints to start the springing action in the rest of the body, the same way a panther pounces on a victim. The idea has meaning for pleasure skiers because the ankle joints are the key part of the body in skiing. The lack of a fluid, graceful style is the result of stiff ankles. Despite the ancient ski adage, "Bend ze knees," it is primarily not the knees, but supple ankles, which make the difference. Most people don't have any trouble bending their knees. But when you learn to spring forward and recoil from your ankle joints and feet, your skiing will have built-in smoothness and ease from the very beginning.

Rhythm is another factor common to all good skiers. It is one of the things that adds natural grace to ski movements. From your very first time on skis you should try to introduce rhythm into your skiing. You can walk with rhythm, practice exercises in rhythm, learn to turn in rhythm. This will not only make your movements look more fluid, it will actually help you to learn faster. Setting up a rhythm in your turns, for instance, keeps you in motion and keeps your body springing up forward (from the ankles) and down again. To look at it from the opposite view, when you don't ski with rhythm, you tend to become static. The movements become mechanical and abrupt. The legs are more apt to be stiff in the action joints, and then nothing works properly. Some people sing or whistle. Others just count to themselves until they get the feeling of rhythm. If you make a conscious effort to ski with rhythm, it will come naturally to you before long and you'll look and feel better on your skis, even as early in your progress as the snow plow exercise.

It all adds up to this: Pleasure skiing is mostly traversing and turning in a rhythm suited to the terrain you're skiing. The legs and hips will be doing most of the work, with the ankle joints the key to your progress. If you can get your ankles to bend easily and often, your knees will bend too, and you'll find it easy to master the movements that will give you control of your skis.

Chapter Three

GETTING THE FIRST FEEL OF THE SKIS

Stepping Around

What Is It?

Stepping around is a series of small steps, executed by lifting one end of the ski while the other end is stationary.

Why Learn It?

When you're standing on a flat spot *stepping around* is the easiest method of getting around other skiers and objects. It will also enable you to make a complete change of direction. When you're standing on a hill you can step around into the "ready" position for skiing straight downhill.

How to Do It

There are two ways of stepping around. One is to step the ski tips around while the tails remain on the snow. The other is to keep the tips stationary and step the tails around.

Let's step the tips around first. Pretend you're standing on the dial of a large clock, facing the rim. Your skis move with the hands of the clock. The fronts go around while the tails remain on the snow in the center. Starting with the tips of both skis at 12 o'clock, step the tip of the right ski to 1 o'clock. Step the left up to it. Step the right to 2 o'clock. Bring the left up to it. Complete the circle, taking small steps. Now go around the dial counter-clockwise, starting with a step to the left. Once you have completed a few turns in each direction, use your poles for additional balance and support.

The second version is similar, but the tails of the skis switch positions with the tips. Now you're on the clock dial, facing inward. Step the tails around the circle, keeping the tips on the snow. Start

with the tails of both skis at 12 o'clock. Step the tail of the left ski to 1 o'clock. Bring the tail of the right ski alongside. Step the left ski to 2 o'clock. Step the back of the right ski alongside. Continue around the face of the clock until you are facing your original direction. Practice making complete circles in both directions.

Common Mistakes and How to Avoid Them

1. Don't pick the entire ski off the ground. You'll step on your other ski, if you do. Lift one end only.

2. Don't start with the right ski if you want to move to the left. This is a surefire way to cross your skis. If your body is going to move to the left, step the left ski first. If you're going to the right, start with the right ski.

3. Don't try to get all the way around in one or two large steps. Take small steps and keep the lifted end of the ski within 6 inches of the snow. You'll maintain better balance, be more graceful.

4. Don't step the entire ski to the side. There won't be any turning action. Tails must stay put while the tips move around the arc, or vice versa. One end of the skis must remain stationary.

Ideal Terrain to Practice On

Any flat spot where the snow is packed.

Walking on Skis

What Is It?

Walking on skis is almost the same as walking down the street. It is a series of alternating forward steps.

1

4

2

5

Stepping the ski tips around—tails stationary.

3

Why Learn It?

It's the simplest way of getting from one place to another when the terrain is flat. And as a beginner, you'll get the first feel of the weight, size, and maneuverability of the skis from the walking you do.

How to Do It

You won't use your poles at first, so put them on the ground, out of the way. Practice walking without them. Now, pick a specific object or place. Lean forward slightly and start walking toward your objective. Shove your feet forward with a small gliding movement. Don't lift them. Let your arms swing naturally. Keep the skis parallel, as if you were walking on the double line down the middle of a

Stepping the ski tips around—tips stationary.

highway. As you shove the right leg forward, push the right knee toward the tip of the ski so that your weight is on that ski. You'll find that your left arm moves forward with your right ski. As you continue, the left leg moves forward with the right arm. (This alternating leg-to-opposite-arm movement will come naturally, if you just walk and let it happen.) Return to your original spot and slip your hands into the poles. Push your entire hand up through the loop from underneath, then grasp the handle with both straps between thumb and forefinger. Walk in the same manner, keeping the poles pointed directly behind you. As you swing the opposite arm and pole forward, place the point of the pole in the snow ahead of the boot and close to the ski.

Common Mistakes and How to Avoid Them

1. Resist the temptation to look down at the skis. Keep your head up. Look where you're going. (It's like driving a car. You must see what is ahead and try to anticipate the actions of others. You don't drive with your eyes on the front wheels, do you?) *Get into the habit of looking out in front.*

2. Don't lift the entire ski into the air when you bring it forward. Instead, slide the ski forward, keeping the front of the ski on the snow.

3. Don't walk open-toed, à la Charlie Chaplin. Your rhythm and balance will be better if you keep the skis parallel.

4. Don't walk like a wooden soldier. Pretend your knees and ankles have just been lubricated. Walk with supple joints.

5. Don't hold onto the poles for dear life. Relax your grip. Let your arms hang at your sides, poles to the rear. They swing forward with each arm motion, and then fall back to the original position.

Ideal Terrain to Practice On

Any flat or almost flat area.

Sliding

What Is It?

Sliding is walking at high speed.

Why Learn It?

You'll be able to move across level ground more quickly. And it's more fun than walking. *Sliding* is good practice for improving your balance.

How To Do It

As in walking on skis, use the same alternating leg-and-opposite-pole movement; but instead of stepping the skis forward, push-slide, glide; push-slide, glide. Here's the action broken into separate movements:

1. With the left ski advanced, push from the right foot and left pole, sliding your left foot and right pole forward.

2. Glide a moment on the forward left ski, placing the right pole in the snow opposite the front of the left boot. Bring up the right foot and left pole.

3. Just before the gliding movement ends, push off from the new back foot (left) and back pole (right).

Common Mistakes and How to Avoid Them

1. *Rigid ankles and knees.* This will hamper your balance, and will make your movements jerky rather than flowing. As you push off the back foot, press your forward knee forward.

2. *Moving the same-side arm and leg forward.* Exaggerate the opposite-arm-to-leg action until you do it properly without thinking about it.

4

3

7

6

Walking on skis.

3. *Placing the pole too far forward in the snow.* You won't be able to push back against it. To get a strong thrust against the pole, your hand must be forward of the basket. The pole must slant backwards.

4. *Too much weight on the tails of the skis.* You'll have difficulty in sliding them. Try leaning forward ever so slightly from the waist and lifting the backs of the skis as you slide them (perhaps one inch off the ground).

5. *Halting stop-and-go movements.* Concentrate on setting up a rhythm; not too rapidly. Push-slide, glide; push-slide, glide. Now add a more powerful thrust and a longer step.

Ideal Terrain to Practice On

Any level area or one with a very slight grade. If it does have a small incline, practice going downhill.

Chapter Four

GETTING UP A SMALL SLOPE

NOW THAT YOU can maneuver your skis with some facility on level ground, you're ready to learn how to climb. There are several easy, practical ways. We recommend that you master the climbing side-step. Then try a different method each time you climb. It isn't necessary to have all of them down pat before you continue on to other things. While you study these different ways of climbing, notice that they all employ the same basic principle: the use of edging to keep you from sliding backward or sideways.

Edging

What Is It?
Edging is the use of the metal edges on the bottom of your skis to get a grip or "bite" on the snow.

Examine the bottoms of your skis. They're flat and smooth. Along the entire length of each side there is a metal edge. When you ski with the bottoms (including the edges) flat on the snow, you slide easily. When you angle the ski, the edges cut into the snow and provide traction (as in climbing), or the ability to carve a turn.

At this point, some of the terms pertaining to your edges should be explained. These are terms you'll see in subsequent pages of this book. Instructors teaching classes will use them. You'll hear them whenever skiers discuss their favorite subject. They are essential to your understanding of edge control.

When you stand looking down at your skis, the edges underneath your big toes are the "inside edges"; the edges underneath the little toes are the "outside edges." This reference relates the edges to each other in their position on the skis. When you're on a hill, the edge on each ski nearest the summit

is the "uphill edge"; the edge on each ski nearest the bottom is the "downhill edge." This reference relates the edges to their position on the slope, and is always changing. Your uphill edges become your downhill edges when you turn and face the opposite direction. The third way of relating your edges to the arc of your turns is explained later on.

Why Learn It?
Your body movements take effect on the snow through your edge control. Specifically, *edging* gives

Inside and outside edges.

Uphill and downhill edges.

skis," as the right edges dig into the snow and the left edges have been lifted off. You should be able to see the lifted edges. Relax and come back to the flat ski position. Now try it to the opposite side. Roll your knees and ankles to the left. You've angled the left edges into the snow. Roll your knees and ankles to each side several times until you can feel the differences between the flat and edged positions. Don't be concerned if you feel awkward in the edged-ski position. As you put it to use in climbing, you'll quickly acquire facility.

Here's an exercise which will prepare you for climbing: *side-stepping* while on your edges. Push your knees and ankles to the right. Staying on the right edges, take 8 side-steps to the right. Look back at the ground you just covered. You'll see the marks where your edges bit into the snow. Roll your knees and ankles to the left. Keeping them bent in that position, side-step to the left until you're back at your original spot. A second set of marks should be apparent. You'll put this exercise to use immediately. Use your poles to help you keep your balance throughout this exercise.

you the ability to climb; it is a key part of making turns; and it provides you with one of the ways to brake your speed.

How to Do It
Stand on level ground and plant both poles in front of you. The entire bottom surface of the skis is on the snow. You are on "flat skis." Push your knees and ankles sharply to the right. You're on "edged

Common Mistakes and How to Avoid Them
1. *Failing to stay on the edge.* Maintain the curved position of your legs with each step. Keep the edges pushed into the snow by pressing your knees to the side.

a) Flat skis.

b) Edged skis.

Fall line.

2. *Trying to take giant steps.* If you get your legs too far apart it will be difficult to stay on the edges. Take small steps.

3. *Edging one ski only.* Be sure you bend both knees and ankles to the side. In order to climb, both skis must grip. Practice edging both in this exercise.

Ideal Terrain to Practice On
Any flat area where the snow is lightly packed.

Climbing Side-Step

What Is It?
The climbing side-step is a method of climbing up a slope, using a combination of movements you have already learned—side-stepping and edging. Side-stepping is your way of moving up the hill. Edging gives you the means of gripping with each step so that you don't slide down.

Why Learn It?
It's a method of climbing most beginners find useful and easy to learn. It's usually the best method for climbing a very steep slope or narrow trail.

How to Do It
You've already learned how to side-step on level ground. And you know how to edge your skis (by rolling your knees and ankles to the side). By side-stepping on the uphill edges of your skis you'll be able to climb directly up the slope.

Time out for a quick explanation of a ski term you will hear often and will need to understand—"fall line." Pretend a friend is standing at the top of a small slope, and he rolls a ball down. In rolling down the ball leaves an imaginary line. This is the shortest, steepest way down the slope, and it is the line that offers least resistance to your skis. In ski parlance it's called the "fall line." Think about where the fall line is on each slope. Try to feel it. With practice, you should be able to do this instinctively, which will speed your progress. You will want to use the fall line to your own advantage and pleasure (skiing into the fall line to pick up speed; away from it to cut your speed). To do this you must know where the fall line is.

The climbing side-step is done with your skis across the fall line so that you're climbing sideways up the slope. Think of it this way. You want to cut a staircase up the fall line, using the edges of your skis. Starting with the ski nearest the top of the hill, take a small step to the side, stomping the upper edge forcefully into the snow. Shift your weight to that ski by bringing your head and body directly over the ski and straightening out the knee. Bring up the lower ski and step it forcefully into the snow on the upper edge with both knees bent. Push off from this bottom ski and side-step the upper ski one more small step up the staircase. Again, stomp the ski into the snow on its edge. Now step the lower ski alongside, also on the edge again, bending both knees. That's all there is to it. Step, together, step, together; always jamming the upper edges into the snow. The harder the snow, the more firmly you stomp your edges. Use your poles for balance. Place them in the snow just opposite the front of your boot. When the terrain is shallow, the poles move with the opposite leg. When the slope is steep and you need extra

Cutting a staircase up the fall line.

support, the upper pole moves with the upper ski, lower pole with the lower ski.

Common Mistakes and How to Avoid Them

1. *Stepping on flat skis and/or using the downhill edge.* If your first step is too big, you'll probably put the lower edge into the snow, or you'll put the ski flat on the slope. When you try to put weight on it, your leg will slide down to your starting point. Take small steps. You'll find it easier to keep your knees and ankles pressed toward the top of the hill; and it will be easier to get the upper edges pushed into the snow.

2. *Not keeping the skis parallel.* In taking a step with the upper ski, if you swing the tip too far uphill, you'll slide back and cross ski tails. If you step the tail higher than the tip, you'll slide forward. To prevent crossing the skis and/or slipping down the slope, keep your skis parallel and across the slope.

3. *Not bringing the lower ski close alongside the upper ski.* This results in taking many more climbing steps than necessary to reach your objective. The action of climbing is step, together, step, together. In making the upward step, your starting point is a push-off from the lower ski. So bring the lower ski as high up the hill as possible each time.

4. *Placing the poles too far forward or too far back.* Your poles should be just in front of your boots. If you place them too far in front of your bindings, when you lean on them you will be forward on the skis. If you place them behind your boots, you will be back on the skis. With your poles just in front of your boots you'll be centered over the skis and properly balanced.

Ideal Terrain to Practice On

A small slope, not too steep—preferably one away from the main area.

Uphill Traverse

What Is It?

The uphill traverse consists of walking diagonally up a slope. You'll learn it easily because it is a combination of movements you've already practiced; that is, walking and edging.

Why Learn It?

When you want to go to a point up and across a hill the uphill traverse is an easy way to climb. Although it can be done on hills of all degrees of steepness, the uphill traverse works best on gradual and medium slopes.

How to Do It

Begin on level ground, near a gentle grade. Walk diagonally toward the crest of the hill. As you start to go up, press your knees and ankles toward the top of the hill so that your upper edges dig into the snow. Keep walking with both skis edged. Use your poles for added support. Hold your poles over the top. That is, cup the palms of your hands over the top of the handles. With every step keep the basket of the pole behind the foot so that you can push yourself forward. Make sure that you walk with the skis parallel and comfortably close together.

Common Mistakes and How to Avoid Them

1. *Taking steps that are too big.* The result is that you will have difficulty making forward progress. Take small steps. It will be easier for you to stay centered and balanced over the skis. It will also be easier to shift from one ski to the other.

2. *Leaning your head and body into the hill.* You'll lose your balance for sure. Press only the knees and ankles uphill. Keep your head over the skis.

3. *Walking with stiff knees and ankles.* Remember your normal walking motions. Knees and ankles

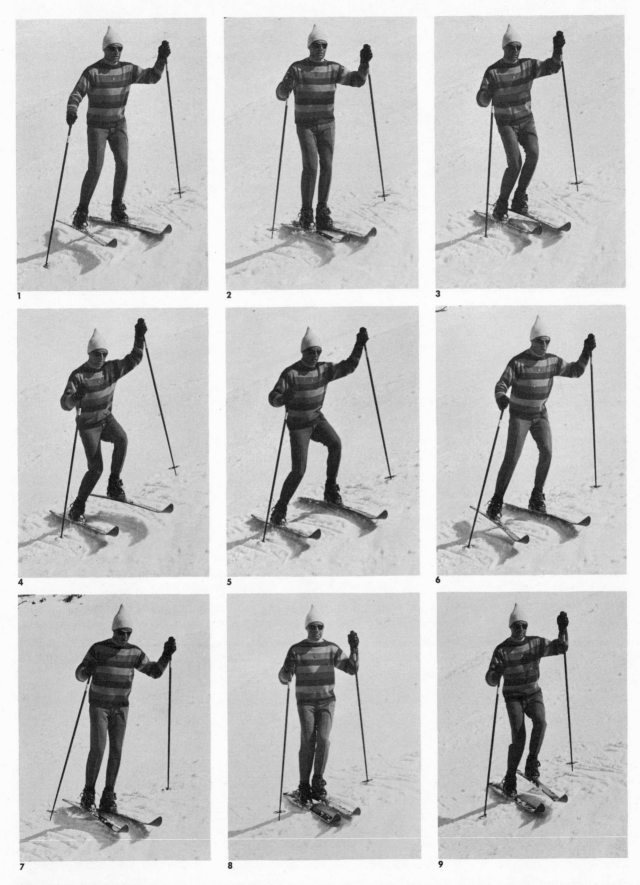

Sequence in climbing side-step.

Diagonal side—step.

are supple. Without this looseness, you'll be mechanical rather than graceful.

4. *Watching the skis.* Hold your head up to see what's in front and who's coming down. Looking at your feet is a habit to be avoided. It hinders your progress, and you endanger yourself when you walk across a slope without being aware of the activity around you.

5. *Walking on flat skis.* You'll slide sideways down the hill. The entire key to climbing is edging, so keep the skis tilted into the slope.

Ideal Terrain to Practice On
A slope that has a moderate grade, preferably one that is wide so that you can make a gradual diagonal ascent. If the hill is too narrow, your ascent will be steeper and more tiring.

Diagonal Side-Step

What Is It?
The diagonal side-step is another way to climb a slope, combining walking with the side-step.

a) Position of hands on poles for normal usage.

b) Position of hands on poles for maximum support.

Why Learn It?

The *diagonal side-step* is less tiring than side-stepping directly up the fall line. (Your legs have forward motion.) And it's a good way to climb a wide open slope or trail.

How to Do It

Start on a gradual slope. Walk diagonally uphill with the uphill traverse. After a few steps, lift the uphill ski forward and sideways at the same time. Plant it firmly across the fall line. Bring the lower ski up close to it. Walk another step forward and upward at the same time. Bring the lower ski close alongside. The action becomes step forward-uphill, together. Step forward-uphill, together. When the terrain is shallow, the poles move with the opposite leg, as in walking. When the slope is steep and you need the extra support, the upper pole moves with the upper ski, lower pole with the lower ski, as in side-stepping.

Common Mistakes and How to Avoid Them

Basically the same mistakes as those made by skiers learning the uphill traverse or the side-step. See those pages.

Ideal Terrain to Practice On

A wide open area with a moderate grade. After you feel comfortable climbing here, then try it on a steeper hill.

Herringbone

What Is It?

Herringbone is a method of climbing, using the inside edges of your skis to prevent slipping back. Skis leave a herringbone pattern in the snow.

Why Learn It?

The *herringbone* is a good way to climb directly up the fall line. It is particularly practical for beginners: they can use it to climb up the side of a slope well out of the way of skiers coming down, without having to cross it. It is tiring, though, for long steep ascents. Use it for short climbs only.

How to Do It

Start on level ground just in front of a slope. Open your skis into a small V position by spreading the tips a little. Keep the tails together. Press your knees slightly toward the inside so that your weight is on the inside edges. Practice walking around on your inside edges, skis in the V. Look back at your tracks. You should be able to see distinct edge marks in the snow. Walk forward toward the hill keeping the V position. Continue walking directly up the hill, opening the front of your skis. Push your poles into the snow behind the boots, palms over the top of the grip. As the slope gets steeper, spread the tips wider. Stamp the edges into the snow with more vigor. Your upper body leans up the hill, making it easier for you to lift your legs. As in walking, move your poles with the opposite leg. Remember, your objective is to walk straight up the hill on your inside edges. Lift your left ski forward as you push from the left pole and the right ski. Put your weight on the left ski. Lift your right ski forward and up the slope, pushing from the right pole and left ski. The trick is to lift the ski just high enough to clear the tail of the other ski and then bring it directly forward.

Common Mistakes and How to Avoid Them

1. *Losing the V position of the skis*. When you spread the tips be sure the tails stay close together. Then turn your knees in toward the snow. As you begin to climb, think of lifting the foot *in that same open-toed position,* directly uphill.

2. *Not using the poles to push yourself up the slope*. First, wrap the palms of your hands over the end of the handle. You get better support holding your poles this way. Keep the poles behind your boots. To take a climbing step with the right leg, thrust simultaneously with the right pole and left leg.

3. *Stepping on the backs of your skis*. Lift first, then bring the ski uphill. These motions seem almost like two separate actions but they'll blend into one with more experience.

4. *Lifting the ski too high*. You'll find it takes much less effort and fewer steps if you think about lifting low, then stepping far. Your progress is determined by how far up the hill you can comfortably step the ski.

Ideal Terrain to Practice On

Any hill that has a level area at the bottom and isn't too steep or too long—and preferably is out of the way of the mainstream of skiers.

Kick Turn

What it Is

A method of making an about-face turn in one step, from a stationary position, by kicking one ski into the air to change its direction.

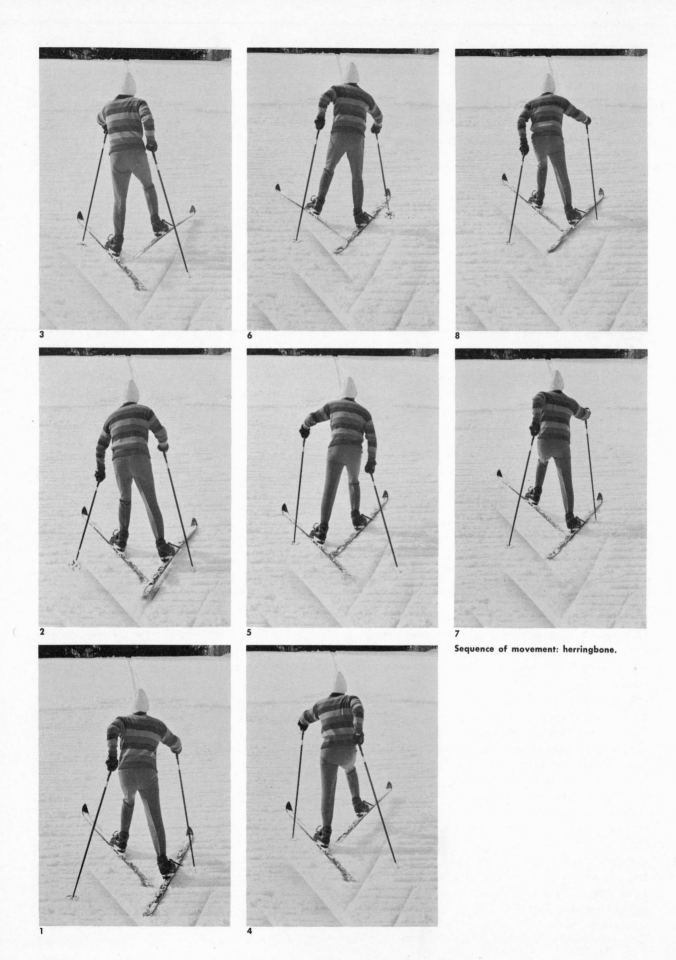

3

6

8

2

5

7

Sequence of movement: herringbone.

1

4

Why Learn It?

For use on level ground, the *kick turn* provides a quick means of making a complete change of direction. On slopes, it is often the most practical way of turning around when you're standing still. The steeper the slope the more practical it is to use the kick turn to turn around.

How to Do It

The kick turn seems awkward at first because the kicking part of the turn is unlike anything you've experienced so far. Let's build up to the complete turn by first practicing some of the individual movements involved.

Find a level area that is not icy. Stand with your feet a few inches apart, skis parallel. Plant your poles just forward of your boots, close enough to the skis so that you can use them for support. The first movement to practice is this: using the pole to help you stay balanced, swing one ski backward, keeping the ski tip on the snow but lifting the tail into the air. Bend slightly forward at the waist as you swing the leg back. Return to your original position. Swing the leg back. Return to your original position. After 4 or 5 swings with each leg, practice the following variation: again using your poles for support, swing one leg backward and then immediately forward until you have swung the entire ski into the air and it is in a vertical position, with the tail of the ski sitting on the snow. Immediately lift it and let it slide back to your original position. This is not an exercise to see how long you can balance on the one leg, so don't stand with your ski vertical for more than a split second. The purpose of the exercise is to give you the feel of swinging your ski backward and then forward until you're able to place the tail of the ski into the snow alongside your stationary ski. To kick one ski into the air, you must put all your weight on the other ski. Keep the knee of that stationary leg bent and you will have better balance. After you have kicked each ski into the upright position 5 or 6 times, you should be ready to do the complete turn.

While you're still on level ground, get comfortable in your standing position. Slide your hands over the ends of your ski pole grips so that your palms cup the top of the poles. You'll get more support from the poles when you hold them in this manner. Now place the left ski pole forward near the tip of your left ski, and the right pole just behind the right ski. Look forward. Put your weight entirely on your left leg and left arm. The right arm carries a little weight but is used mostly to help you stay balanced at this point. Swing your right ski backward (leave the ski tip on the snow but raise the tail) and immediately swing it forward into the air. Set the ski tail into the snow near the tip of the left ski. Without hesitation turn your right knee out so that the right ski tip will fall around into the new direction. It should be parallel to your stationary ski and only a few inches from it. Turn your head and shoulders and look toward the new direction, leaning on the right pole. You can then pick up your left ski, your left pole, and step the entire left side around. Set the left ski down alongside the right ski as you put the left pole into the snow in front of your left boot.

To make a kick turn using the left leg as the turning side, plant your right pole forward, your left pole to the rear. Take a comfortable stance with all your weight on the right leg and right arm. Slide the left ski back; then slide it all the way forward and into the air. Set the tail end of the ski into the snow, close to the right ski tip. Immediately turn the left ski tip around by turning your left knee out. Let the left ski fall into the snow. It should be parallel to your right ski, but facing in the opposite direction. Now twist your head and shoulders and look in the new direction. Lean on the left pole. This frees your right side of weight, so that you can step the right ski around while you bring the pole around too. Place the right ski alongside the left. Put the right pole into the snow.

These are the main points to remember about kick turns:

1. You'll be balancing on one leg. Be sure that you have a firm stance on that leg.

2. Swing your turning leg *back* before you swing it forward. It gives you a little momentum and makes it easier to kick all the way into the upright position.

3. Immediately turn your knee out. The ski tip will automatically turn into the new direction and fall into place.

4. Twist your upper body into the new direction and lean on the pole on that side. The other side will have no weight on it and you'll find it easy to step that ski around into position.

To make a kick turn on a slope, you use the exact same movements, but there are a few things you must do in addition. Because you're on a hill, you must insure your stationary position by standing with your skis directly across the fall line. Stamp your uphill ski firmly into the snow so that you can stand on it solidly. Then kick your downhill leg and turn out your knee. Make sure the downhill ski falls into position directly across the fall line also, before you transfer your weight to it. If your downhill ski is not across the fall line, when you shift your weight

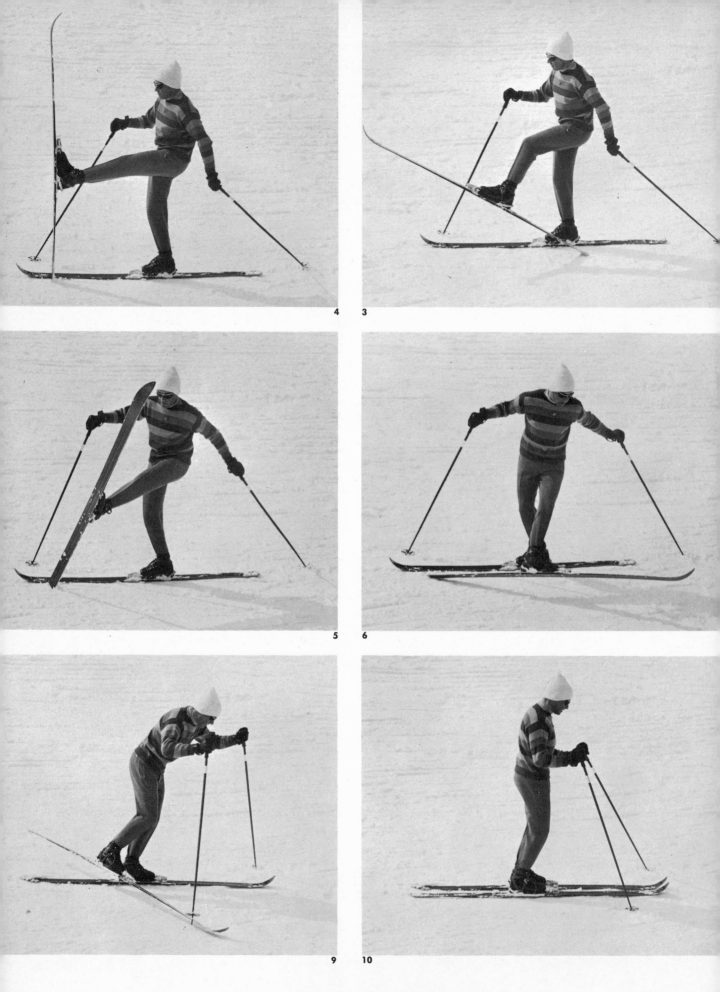

2 **1**

7 **8**

Sequence of movement: kick turn.

to it, you will start to move downhill whether you're ready or not.

If the slope is very steep there is another way of using your poles, which makes the kick turn easier. Instead of putting the downhill pole into the snow just behind the downhill ski, and the stationary side pole forward (as we told you to do previously), try this instead: Hold both poles close to your sides, hands at armpit height. Now turn your head, upper body, and arms to face downhill. Your poles should be across your skis with the tips pointing into the slope. Push both tips into the snow (above the uphill ski) and lean uphill on them. Now there is little if any weight on your downhill leg. It's free to be kicked into the air, and turned in the new direction. Be sure the turned ski is directly across the fall line,

with the edge into the snow. Turn your head and upper body in the new direction and bring them over the turned ski so that your weight will be automatically shifted to the turned ski. Balancing on the turned ski, swing the uphill ski around at the same time you bring your uphill arm and pole around.

Kick turns on a hill can also be made by kicking the uphill ski. We recommend kicking the downhill ski, which most people find easier.

Common Mistakes and How to Avoid Them

1. *Not starting in a position with a secure footing.* In order to be able to stay balanced on one leg while you're kicking the other into the air, you have to be standing firmly on the snow. The area under your foot should give you solid support. When you're first

35

Position of skis when making kick turn on a slope.

practicing, try to find level even patches of snow. If you're on a hill, be sure your edges (uphill) have a good bite.

2. *Not swinging the leg back first before kicking it forward into the air.* It's so much easier to swing the leg and ski into the air if you have built up some momentum on the back swing. After you bring the ski back, don't hesitate. Swing it forward on the ground as far as it will go and then up into the air.

3. *Turning the ski into the new direction while it's completely in the air.* You can change the direction of the ski with your leg while it is in the air, but you'll have trouble placing it parallel, and close alongside your stationary ski. Do it the easy way. Put the tail of the kick ski into the snow close to the tip of the stationary one. Turn out your knee and the vertical ski will swing down into the snow close alongside.

4. *Not transferring your weight to the ski that you* *have kick turned before stepping the other ski around.* You'll probably be unable to move. To step the other ski around and complete the turn, you have to take your weight off it. Do this by twisting your head and shoulders in the new direction. Lean on the pole on that side. This frees your opposite side. The leg, ski, and arm will come around easily.

5. *Placing the poles into the snow too far from (or too close to) your body.* Your poles provide essential support during the kick turn. If they're too far from your body you won't be able to get your hand positioned above the basket so that you can lean on the pole at the proper time. If they're too close to your body, they'll interfere with the movement of your skis.

Ideal Terrain to Practice On
A level area covered with snow that is packed but not icy.

1   2   3

6   5   4

Kick turn on a very steep slope.

7

Chapter Five

COMING DOWN

YOU'VE GOTTEN to the top of this small slope. Good. You're ready to experience the first exhilarating sensation of downhill motion. One of the great things about skiing is that the wonderful excitement doesn't become old hat; and as you gain more and more control of the skis, your joys will multiply.

Downhill Running

What Is It?
Downhill running is the position you use when skiing straight down a hill. It's sometimes called "schussing" position, although schussing refers to high-speed straight-downhill running.

Why Learn It?
The *downhill running* position will enable you to ski down with maximum balance. It is one of the Basic Ski Positions. Since many subsequent maneuvers are based on it, it's well worth your while to spend extra time getting to feel comfortable doing it.

How to Do It
Practice on level ground first. Here is the position you want to feel. Stand erect with your feet a comfortable 3 or 4 inches apart, skis parallel, either one slightly advanced. Lower your hips straight down toward your toes. This forces your ankles and knees to bend. Bend your ankles and knees, *not your waist*. Lift your arms forward so that with elbows bent, your hands are at your waistline. Your poles are held with the baskets to the rear of your body, about a foot above the snow. Now lift your head up and look in front of you. Relax and you're set to glide down the hill. Take a deep breath from the waistline.

Downhill running position.

Loosen your death grip on the poles. Gently bob up and down in the legs, pushing up ever so lightly from the balls of the feet. Smile. This is your downhill running position.

Important: Since you have not yet learned how to make any of the stop turns, be sure to practice on a slope that has a long, level run-out. You'll come to a stop as you run out of momentum. If the flat

38

1

2

3

6

5

4

7

Starting from part way up the hill.

area isn't very big, practice from only part way up the hill.

Here's an easy way to get into a comfortable starting position. If the top of the hill is flat, walk over to the edge and stop. Plant both poles in the snow near your feet. Assume the downhill running position. *Relax,* take a deep breath, bob from the balls of the feet, loosen your grip on poles, and smile. Unstick your skis by shuffling them back and forward before you start. Push yourself forward. As you start to move, lift your arms slightly forward to keep your poles from dragging in the snow.

If you're starting from part way up the hill, sidestep up to your starting point. With skis directly across the fall line, walk out across so that you're not too close to any obstacles along the side. Turn your head and shoulders to the bottom of the hill. Plant both poles below you, shoulder-width apart. Lean on the poles so that you don't start down until you're actually ready. (Keep the poles at waist level, hands over the tops of the handle.) Step-turn the tails of your skis, taking small steps, so that your ski tips are between the poles and you are facing directly down the hill. When you're not accustomed to it, this starting position is tough on the arms. So don't drag out the procedure. The longer you stand, the harder it becomes to stay supple. Unstick your skis by shuffling them back and forward before you start.

Common Mistakes and How to Avoid Them

1. *Rigid ankles.* This produces a chair-sitting position, where you are bent in the knees and waist, instead of the ankles and knees. To correct it, stand erect to eliminate the excess waist-bend. Then pump your knees straight down toward the front of the skis. (The knees must be in front of the ankles so that the shinbone slants back.) Spring up and down lightly from the feet.

2. *Looking down at the skis.* Stand erect with your head up. Now sink into your ankle- and knee-bend. It is a great temptation to watch your skis. But looking at them doesn't help one bit. In fact, it's a definite hazard to your safety as well as a hindrance to your progress.

3. *Catching the outside edge of your ski.* This happens when you're not standing squarely over both skis; or when you bow your legs, cowboy style. Remember, keep your head directly over your skis. Bend your knees to the tips only—not sideways—so that you are riding flat skis.

4. *Hanging too far forward.* This exaggerated position doesn't afford good balance, either. Well-meaning friends may have advised you to "get out in front" of your skis. They were probably trying to encourage you not to sit back. You'll maintain better balance if you don't try to force your nose out over the front of your skis. Just push your hips down toward your toes. You'll be slightly forward, yet the heels of your boots will be touching the skis.

5. *Standing rigidly on the skis.* This means stiff ankles, stiff knees, taut arms, no fun. Try starting lower down the hill, practicing until you can come down with some looseness in your body. *Relax* before starting down (relax your grip on the poles, take a deep breath, bob lightly in the legs, *smile*). And here's another trick you might try. Sing aloud. Even if you're not Sinatra or Dinah, singing has a tendency to relax you.

Ideal Terrain to Practice On

A smooth hill that has a gradual slope and is not too long. (Remember you'll be climbing back up.) It should have a flat run-out at the bottom that's at least twice as long as the part you'll be skiing down. If you can find one that has a flat starting place at the top, or even part way up, you'll be able to spend more time practicing downhill running and less time getting ready.

Running Across Small Bumps

What Is It?

Running across small bumps is a way to maintain your balance as you come down a slope that's not smooth.

Why Learn It?

Many slopes you'll be skiing are uneven. They have bumps, ridges, hollows. This lesson will help you learn to maintain your balance as you ride over bumpy terrains. And it will improve your coordination.

How to Do It

The basic principle is simple. All the work is done in the ankles and knees. Use your ankle and knee joints as an auto uses shock absorbers. Have you ever driven in an old tin lizzie? Every little stone in the road jars the passengers. In a Cadillac (or almost any other new car), you sail smoothly along, oblivious of such minor road bumps. Why? The wheels bob up and down on the shock absorbers while the body of the car continues undisturbed at the same level. When you ski with loose, "well oiled" ankles and knees, your body will move forward on an even plane as your legs compress and expand underneath. If you have been bobbing when you practiced downhill running, then you already know the springing action. Now you want to time this action to the contour of the slope.

Practice running over a single bump first. Starting in your normal running position, fairly erect, ski toward the bump. As you approach it, "let" the bump push your ankles and knees up into the bent position. The amount of leg bend is greatest when you get to the crest of the bump. As you come over the bump, your body continues forward and your legs straighten up. Force your legs down to the slope.

(Opposite) Sequence in running bumps.

In other words, let the bump compress your legs. Expand them again after you come over the top of the bump. And at all times, try to keep your body riding at the same level. You'll feel the coordination and the timing more easily if you practice at slow speed.

Common Mistakes and How to Avoid Them

1. *Crouching before you get to the bump.* This prevents your legs from absorbing the bump because there isn't any more "give" left in the joints when you reach it. Approach the bump with your legs only slightly bent. Then they can bend into a deeper position as you get to the top.

2. *Absorbing bumps entirely in the waist.* Try to keep the waist-bend to a minimum so that the upper body rides smoothly as the adjusting to the terrain is done by your lower body. You'll have better balance this way, so keep your head up and let your legs go up and down.

3. *Running stiff-legged.* This will send you off the crest into the air, and it is not advised at this stage when you're learning to use the ankle and knee joints as cushions. Be loose-legged.

4. *Straightening up too soon.* This will also send you flying. Don't straighten out your legs until you're starting down the far side of the bump.

5. *Sitting back.* As in normal smooth slope downhill running, this happens when you squat on the skis. All the bend is in your knees and waist and there is none in your ankles. Correct this by practicing in an upright position with as much bend as you can get from your ankles. Knee-bend will follow automatically, once the ankles bend. Another cause of sitting back is allowing your arms to fall behind your body. Be sure to carry your arms in front of you, as in your regular running position.

Ideal Terrain to Practice On

Look for the same characteristics as you did when you were looking for a slope on which to learn downhill running—not too steep, long flat run-off at the bottom, plus some bumps. Most probably you'll find there are some bumps on your downhill running slope. This time don't pick a line which avoids them. Practice skiing over them.

Falling

Falling is a part of learning to ski. Everyone who skis, including Olympic champions, top instructors, expert weekenders—all occasionally find themselves in the snow. It's no disgrace to take a spill.

If you're a beginner, you can expect to take your share of tumbles—and then perhaps a few more. The sooner you accept this reality, the quicker you'll be able to concentrate fully on your coordination and the contour of the slope. Don't let the fear or embarrassment of falling fill your mind. There are other things on which to focus your attention.

Falling safely is an art, but since any spill is potentially dangerous, we don't advise you to practice falling. Instead, think about and understand the following principles of safe falling. Then apply them to the spills you'll be taking when skiing and learning other maneuvers.

1. *Don't fight the fall all the way down.* Naturally, try not to fall. If you're tottering and can recover your balance—with a quick assist from your poles— do so. As a matter of fact, it helps your confidence and your coordination each time you do. But when you see that you can't regain your position, let go and fall. Try to relax. Admittedly, this is easier said than done; but it can become part of your automatic reaction if, each time you start to go down, you don't wait too long before you try to loosen up.

2. *Try to keep your legs together and your skis parallel.* Your legs will then support each other, and the skis will not try to go in different directions.

3. *Lean backwards and to the side* so that you'll absorb the impact with the most padded part—the rump.

4. *Get your poles out of the way.* Lift your hands in front of your body, so that there is little chance of injury from the points. The poles won't catch on branches or other objects, either.

5. *Don't roll up into a ball.* Your body is better able to resist twisting movements if you fall with your legs extended.

6. *Go with the fall,* particularly in falls where you are being pitched forward (the kind of spill that occurs when your ski tips cross, or you hit an unseen piece of rock, or one ski tip digs in). This type of header usually happens quickly, giving you virtually no chance to recover. Don't fight your momentum. Go with it.

7. *Keep your eyes open.* When you can see what's happening, you have a chance to react. Your balance is better. Closing your eyes robs you of any possibility of helping yourself.

8. After you've taken a header, catch your breath. *Then immediately get up and out of the way of other skiers coming down.* If you punched a hole in the slope (called a "sitzmark"), be sure to fill it in. Otherwise, you'll be creating a hazard for those who ski down afterwards.

1

2

3

4

Fall to the side and rear, keeping legs together.

Getting Up

The two most important things to know about picking yourself out of the snow are: *You must be in the proper position before you try* and then, when you are ready, *you must use your legs for most of the lifting.*

If you are on level ground, here's how to prepare yourself and get up: Put your skis close together, facing in the same direction. (If one ski is caught or they're facing opposite directions, roll over onto your back and unscramble them in the air.) Draw your feet

up as close as possible underneath your seat. Hold both poles in one hand, halfway down. Place them in the snow near your heels on the side of the skis opposite your body. Put your free hand underneath your derrière and push yourself sideways so that you're over the skis. Straighten out your legs as you continue to push down on the poles and your hand.

It will be a little easier once you get into position if you're on a hill. Swing both skis down below you. Wiggle your body around until your head, hips, and

1   2

4   3

5   6

Sequence in getting up.

feet are aligned down the hill. Set your skis directly across the fall line. Draw your feet up as close as possible underneath your seat. With your downhill hand hold the shafts of both poles, which are placed with the tips in the snow below your heels. Your uphill hand is underneath your seat. Push yourself over your skis by pushing away from the hill. Now you can lift from the legs as you continue to push hard against the slope.

If you've fallen into deep, soft snow, use the same actions described above, but use your poles differently. Hold them in the middle of the shaft. Instead of pushing down against the baskets, place the poles flat on the snow and push down against the entire length of the shaft.

Common Mistakes and How to Avoid Them

1. *Starting from the chair-sitting position (hips behind the feet.)* This will be your finishing position, too. Push and the chair moves forward. As energetically as you struggle, you'll be unable to get your hips above the feet, and you won't be able to right yourself. It's essential that your head be opposite your feet when you begin.

2. *Placing the free hand too far away from the derrière.* This cuts the amount of effective push you can generate. Put the hand underneath your back pocket.

3. *Arising while skis are pointed uphill.* You're in for a surprise. You'll slide backward the moment you put weight on the skis. Keep your skis across the fall line to avoid sliding.

Holding the poles for getting up out of deep, soft snow.

4. *Getting up with the skis pointed downhill.* You'll slide downhill while you're still in the process of getting up. In order to remain stationary, your skis must be directly across the fall line.

Chapter Six

LEARNING TO CONTROL THE SKIS

UNTIL NOW, you've been a passenger on the skis. Standing on them—a little nervously no doubt—you rode them down the hill and across the run-out until your momentum expired. Then they stopped, and so did you. Fun? Sure. But think how much more delightful it will be when you're the driver. That's the objective from here on—to help you become master of your skis.

Snowplow

What Is It?

The snowplow is a downhill skiing position in which the tips are close together, and the tails spread apart. From the head-on view, your skis look like a V-shaped snowplow, or like the bow of a boat cutting the water.

Why Learn It?

1. You'll use the *snowplow position* when learning your first turns.

2. It gives you valuable edge control experience while you're in motion downhill.

3. It enables you to check speed without changing direction. That's why racers use it. As a beginner, you are advised to use it as a braking maneuver only when skiing slowly. There are better ways for you to slow down when you're going at a moderate clip (skiing away from the fall line, making a series of turns, and making parallel checks); all these are covered in later chapters.

Important: The snowplow and the snowplow turn are useful maneuvers. They are part of the progression of movements that will lead you to parallel skiing. *Don't be content with the snowplow as your only means of turning and braking.* Although these maneuvers are more than exercises, they should not be thought of as goals in themselves. Learn them so that you can build from them to turns that are more graceful, and that require less effort.

How to Do It

Try this first on level ground, then down the fall line of a gradual slope. Spread the tails of your skis, keeping the tips close, but not touching. Press your ankles and knees forward, then inward. This tilts your skis onto the inside edges. Your upper body

Snowplow position.

46

Increasing the braking effect.

remains almost erect. Arms are carried in front, comfortably away from your body, as if resting on an elbow-high table. Poles point to the rear. You should be positioned directly over the middle, equally balanced between both skis.

After you've gotten into this posture several times, try it down the fall line of a gentle slope. Before you start down, check your position. Are you square between both skis? Tails spread apart? Skis edged in? Look ahead. Take a deep breath, smile, and off you go.

To get more braking effect, increase the pressure on the edges by pushing your hips straight down, spreading the tails wider and increasing the edge bite.

The snowplow is a somewhat awkward position. You're applying constant pressure to the inside edges as you force the tails apart. It's tough on the legs. (Aren't you glad you preconditioned?) But it's the foundation of your first turns. Become adept in this position and the turns will come easily.

Common Mistakes and How to Avoid Them

1. *Not enough edging.* Riding flat skis opposes the very purpose of the snowplow, which is to apply constant pressure to the edges. Bend your knees and ankles in toward the ground and your edges will bite.

2. *Too much edging.* Most common among the girls who tend to push their knees together until they are touching. Instead of brushing the snow, your skis

will run along the edges and cross in front. Don't press your legs so close together. Feel the proper amount of edging by experimenting.

3. *Skis running parallel.* Lose the V position and you lose the braking effect. Regain it by forcing the backs of the skis apart. Keep them wider than the tips.

4. *Bending one leg more than the other.* You're no longer centered between the skis. One ski will be edged, the other flat. The most probable result is that your skis will cross, in front. Correct this by using both legs equally as if they were part of a single unit.

5. *Excessive waist-bend.* This will be a tough habit to break. Don't let it become one. Pick your head up and keep it over your hips. See what is going on in front of you. As in most other ski positions, the bend should be in your ankles and knees.

6. *Protruding derrière.* Pull it in by thrusting your pelvis forward.

7. *Freezing-up.* This happens when your arms are pressed tight against your body and your legs are stiff as a statue's. It is usually accompanied by a look of terror. To correct *relax* (take a deep breath, loosen the death grip on the poles, lighten your ankles, bob your knees, and *smile*).

Ideal Terrain to Practice On

Any gentle hill that has packed snow—preferably one with a level starting point and a run-out at the bottom.

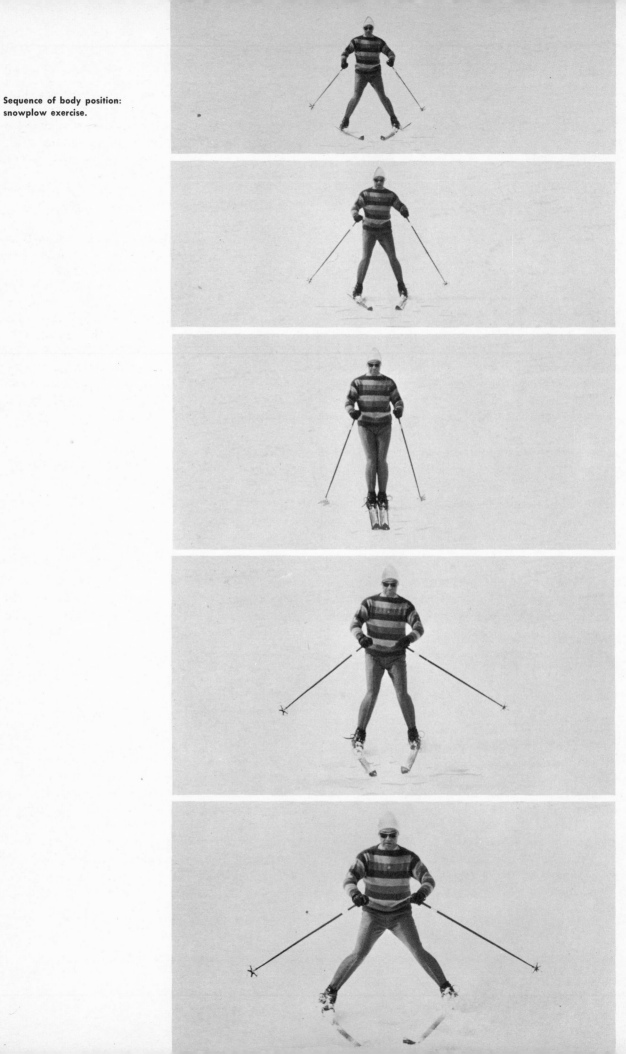

Sequence of body position:
snowplow exercise.

Snowplow Exercise

What Is It?

In the snowplow exercise you alternate your position between the snowplow and your normal running position while skiing down the fall line.

Why Learn It?

The *snowplow exercise* will help you feel the braking effect of edging. It will help you learn to snowplow without freezing in one position; it will prepare you for turning; and it will improve your balance.

How to Do It

You'll need a long, gradually sloping hill to practice this one. While you're standing at the top, get set in the proper snowplow. Push off directly down the hill and ski a short distance in the snowplow. Raise your body up and forward (push up from the feet and partly straighten out the legs), letting your skis come together underneath you. Ski in this schuss position a short way and then push back into the snowplow (force your heels out, lower your hips, and edge the skis in). Make the change from one position to the other several times on each run.

On your next practice run, try it by starting in the straight running position and pushing into the snowplow. After you've practiced it a few times, *try to introduce a rhythm into the exercise*.

Common Mistakes and How to Avoid Them

1. *Picking up too much speed in the schuss position.* Don't get going full blast before starting into your snowplow. The speed will preoccupy you. You'll find it difficult to make the change.

2. *Not returning to an edged snowplow.* Be sure you're changing from flat, parallel skis to edged, V-position skis. Roll your ankles in slightly when you force the backs of the skis to the outside.

3. *Not bringing the tips together in the plow.* Instead of pushing the feet apart (which spreads the entire skis but keeps them parallel) concentrate on pushing your heels apart. This will spread the tail end of the skis only.

Ideal Terrain to Practice On

A very long, gentle hill, smooth rather than bumpy.

Chapter Seven

YOUR FIRST TURNS

YOU'RE ON THE THRESHOLD. Once you've made your first turns while actually moving down the hill, you will have crossed over into a new realm of ski experience. With each new descent, your sense of accomplishment and satisfaction will swell.

To make snowplow turns you just apply turning power to your straight snowplow position. If you have learned the snowplow position reasonably well, the turns will come easily. Ask yourself these questions. Can you pick a spot part way down the hill, snowplow at an even speed up to it, then apply your braking action exactly at that spot? Can you make the change from straight running position to snowplow 3 times, within 20 yards from your starting point? When you can, you're ready to learn to turn.

Inside and Outside Ski

Now that you are about to begin making turns, we will introduce a set of terms that will become as familiar to you as "downhill ski" and "uphill ski." The new terms are "inside ski" and "outside ski." The inside ski is the ski on the inside of the turn and the outside ski is the one on the outside of the turn. When you turn to the right, the right ski is the inside ski and the left ski is the outside ski. Similarly, when you turn to the left, the left ski is the inside ski and the right ski is the outside ski.

Turning Power

What Is It?

Skis won't turn by themselves. Turning power creates a force that will turn the skis.

Why Learn It?

This force will produce turns when applied to the various downhill positions you already know (normal running position and the snowplow position), as well as when applied to the traverse position which you'll learn in a few lessons. When you're skiing fast or even moderately fast, you'll use this *turning power* to help you come to a complete stop.

How to Do It

There are two ways to produce turning power. Let's practice them separately. The first is *turning power through lower body rotation*. You won't need your skis or poles to get the first feel of this, so take them off and put them aside. Stand on level ground with your feet about 3 inches apart, knees slightly bent. Pretend there is a lighted cigarette under the front of your boot and you are putting it out. Twist your right foot and turn your heel out. Press down on the foot and turn it at the same time. Naturally your right knee and leg also turn, but the action begins when you swivel your foot. Try it once or twice more, twisting only the right foot to the right. Now move your feet closer together so that they are barely touching. In one motion, sink in the knees and ankles as you sharply swivel both feet to the right. Swivel both feet sharply to the left. Notice how your shoulders are facing a different direction than your legs, as a counterbalance.

Straighten up in the legs and return your shoulders to their normal square position over the hips. Flex your knees slightly and then try it again. There's still a lighted cigarette under the ball of your right

Swivel foot to put out cigarette.

foot which you want to crush. Pivot both feet quickly to the right as you sink into a lower position.

Now let's try it to the opposite direction. Rotate the left foot only, at first. Stand with knees flexed, feet a few inches apart. Swivel the left foot, turning the left heel out. Crush the imaginary cigarette underneath the sole of your left foot. Now do it using both feet. Move them closer together. With a quick motion, drop your hips a few inches as you twist both your feet to the left. Again your shoulders will be facing a different direction than your legs. *This is exactly how your turning power will work when you're on skis.* The turning action of the legs and the sinking action of the hips are simultaneous. Your shoulders will move in the opposite direction.

Practice this exercise at least a dozen times to each side. Then put on your skis (but not your poles yet) and practice swiveling both feet and skis to each side, using the same movements as when you did it without the skis. Practice this on snow that has been smoothed down so that your skis slide around. Try to use as forceful a foot swivel as you can, but don't expect your skis to turn more than 4 or 5 inches now. When you are in motion skiing down the hill, this same amount of turning power will produce a much sharper turn.

The second source of turning power is weight shift from one leg to the other. This is usually used in combination with leg rotation to give you an easy, yet powerful, way to turn your skis. By itself, weight shifting is not as effective. Try it this way to get the first feel of it. The first application of weight shift to turn your skis will be in the snowplow turn, so try it in the snowplow position. Take a snowplow stance with your feet about 18 inches apart. Check to be sure your knees are pushed forward of your ankles. Turn your head and shoulders to the left. Bending sideways slightly from the waist, bring your head and shoulders over the left ski so that your head is directly above the little toe on your left foot. Your left shoulder is drawn back and lowered slightly. You have shifted your weight to the left ski. When you first took the snowplow stance your weight was centered equally between both skis. By changing the position of your upper body so that it moved over to a position above the left ski, you have transferred your weight to that ski.

By shifting your weight to the left ski you have made that ski dominant. Since it is pointing to the right you would be turning to the right. If you were now to transfer your weight all the way over to the right ski, the right ski would control your direction.

 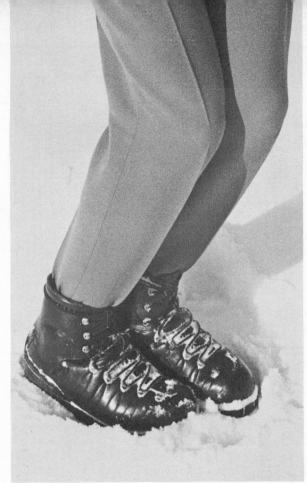

Swiveling both feet—shoulders are not out of line.

Since it's pointing to the left, you would be turning to the left.

When you progress to the point where you're learning more advanced turns (stem, parallel christie, and wedeln) you'll find it a little easier to shift your weight. You'll be skiing with your legs closer together and your upper body won't have so far to travel to help you shift weight. You will also shift your weight by taking very small steps from one ski to the other.

Let's try this stepping method of shifting your weight. Take a narrow snowplow stance (feet about 15 inches apart). Step the right ski alongside the left ski so that both now point to the right. If you move your head and shoulders laterally across at the same time you step the right ski over, you will finish with both skis pointing to the right, and your head and shoulders facing off at an angle to the left. Your left shoulder will be held back. This stepping method is the same method of shifting weight you'll use when you learn the stem christie. Now try it to the opposite side. Start from a narrow comfortable snowplow position. Spring lightly from the ankles once or twice to keep your ankles and knees supple. Step the left ski over alongside the right ski, bringing your head and shoulders directly

above the little toe on your right foot. This time your right shoulder is drawn back. You have shifted your weight to the right ski.

Finally, try shifting your weight as you will when you are learning parallel christies and wedeln. Stand with your skis parallel, your legs pressed lightly together. Keeping them together, hop from one ski to the other, lifting the tail of the opposite ski completely off the snow. This is an exaggerated movement, but you will see how it is possible to remain in a compact position and change your weight from one ski to the other. Now try it a few times without the exaggeration. Hop lightly from one ski to the other without making a conscious effort to lift the tail of the opposite ski completely off the snow. This is very close to the way you'll be using weight shift to learn the advanced turns.

Common Mistakes and How to Avoid Them

LEG ROTATION. 1. *Rigid ankles and knees.* This will prevent your sinking as you swivel your feet, and as a result you'll find it more difficult to actually turn them. Be loose by bobbing lightly up and down from the balls of the feet before you start.

2. *Swinging the fanny.* The movement should be a leg rotation that starts twisting or pivoting your

52

Weight shift in the snowplow position.

Weight shift as it is used in the stem christie.

Weight shift in the compact running position.

feet. Concentrate on pressing down on the balls of the feet and swiveling. The hips will move naturally as a result of the action of the legs.

WEIGHT SHIFTING. 1. *Straightening one or both legs completely*. When you're skiing, and particularly when you're shifting weight, you will be in motion, both sinking into a deeper bend and straightening out again. The trick is *always to have some ankle- and knee-bend*. Don't straighten up completely. When you do, you lose pressure on the front part of the skis and they will separate. To control the skis, you must always maintain some pressure on the part of the skis in front of your boots.

2. *Overexaggerating the upper body lean from the waist*. Turn your head and shoulders so that your chin is directly over your little toe. Only a small break at the waist is needed. The further out you push beyond that point, the greater the distance you'll have to move when you shift to the other side and the more difficult it will be to stay balanced. Remember the basic principle: Economize on your movements. Your skiing will require less effort and you'll be able to balance more gracefully.

Ideal Terrain to Practice On
Any level area.

Snowplow Turn

What Is It?
When you make a snowplow turn you change direction while skiing the entire turn in snowplow position.

Why Learn It?
The *snowplow turn* is a quick way to learn to turn. In snowplow position one ski is always pointing in the direction to which you want to turn. Put weight on that ski and you're already halfway through the turn. The turns are most effective on wide and relatively shallow terrain. In the process of learning this turn, you will learn to shift your weight from one ski to the other as well as to steer with your leg.

But remember—skiing with your skis apart is more awkward than skiing with them parallel and close together. So learn the snowplow turn and then proceed to build the more advanced skiing on the lessons you will learn from it, such as shifting your weight from one ski to the other and steering the skis around by turning the feet and legs.

How to Do It
Your method in learning to make snowplow turns should be as follows: Practice a single right turn at a time. After you've made 3 or 4 single right turns, then practice single turns to the left. After you've made 3 or 4 left turns, utilize the entire length of the slope, and practice linking right and left turns all the way down.

Climb part way up a gentle slope. Turn your head and shoulders downhill. Put your poles into the snow below you. Use them for support. Step your skis around until you're facing directly down the fall-line. Push your knees forward and inward into the snowplow position. Shuffle your skis back and forward so that they're not sticking and will slide easily.

Then push off. Ski straight down for about 10 feet in a good snowplow position. Your weight is centered between the skis. Now begin to apply turning force. Shift your weight to the left ski by bringing your head and shoulders out over the left boot. Leaning out at the waist, lower the left shoulder, and draw it back. Check your position. Look down momentarily. Your eyes should be directly above your little toe. You have transferred your weight to the left ski, and if you have maintained your original snowplow position in both legs, you will be turning to the right. For the turning force of your weight shift to take effect, the inside edge of your left ski must bite into the snow. It should have been biting in your straight snowplow position. In order to help the turn, *increase this edging* by rolling your left knee inward as you bend sideways from the waist and lean out above the left foot. Climb back up and try it again, this time making more positive movements.

As you did on your previous run, ski straight down in the snowplow position; then as you increase your inside edging of the left ski, shift your weight over *against* the left ski. Many instructors have found that you use firmer pressure downward against the edge and get a more effective weight shift if you think of putting your weight *against* the ski instead of merely *on* it. This time, add more turning power by steering the left ski around with your leg. You can do it by pressing down on the left foot and putting out an imaginary cigarette underneath the sole of your left boot. You're actually swiveling or

rotating your left foot, left knee, and entire left leg. See how much sharper the turn is?

After 3 or 4 turns to the right, practice some to the left. Reverse the weight-shifting and foot-steering instructions. You want to make the right ski the controlling ski (because it's pointing to the left), so you bring your head and shoulders out above your right boot, increasing the inside edging of the right ski. Then add more turning power by steering the ski around with a turning movement of the right foot, the right knee, and the entire right leg. Once you've made several individual left turns, link right and left turns together, one after the other. Start with a turn to the right. Just before you complete the turn, momentarily return to the centered position between the skis. Then lean out over the right ski (which will start your turn to the left). Soon you'll be able to move from the lean-out turning position on one side to the lean-out turning position on the other side without the intermediary return to the centered position. *Keep the snowplow position of the legs and skis throughout the turns.*

Common Mistakes and How to Avoid Them

1. *Straightening out the knee of the unweighted leg.* That ski will lag behind and then the tips will cross. The shifting of weight by bringing your head and shoulders over one of the skis is an *upper* body movement. Both legs remain in the snowplow position, both ankles and knees bent.

2. *Flattening out the weighted ski.* The flat ski cancels out the effect of the turning power, which works only when the inside edge of the weighted ski grips the snow. Instead of turning, you'll be sliding sideways. When you transfer your weight over to one ski, roll that knee inward to increase your edge bite.

3. *Too much forward waist-bend.* This is usually followed by stiffening legs, loss of snowplow position in the skis, and a tumble instead of a turn. Start with the upper body almost erect. There is no forward waist-bend. When you transfer your weight to one ski, by leaning out over the boot, there is only a *sideways* bend in the waist.

4. *Leading with the outside shoulder* (the shoulder over the weighted ski). This throws the entire upper body out of position. The result is that your head (which should be over the weighted ski), usually ends up over the inside (unweighted) ski. The turn can be made in this position. In effect, the turning power is a rotation of the shoulders instead of weight shift and foot-turning. Shoulder rotation, as a source of turning power, is not as efficient. Too often it leads to leaning into the hill instead of away from the hill. Keep the outside shoulder lowered and slightly drawn back.

5. *Letting the tips of the skis spread apart.* The skis tend to run parallel, without turning. The snowplow position of the skis is effective because each ski points in a new direction. Shift weight over to that ski and it starts turning, already halfway through the turn. You lose that advantage if you don't keep the tips close together. How can you keep them there? Force the heels of your boots to the outside. This will push the tails of the skis apart and keep the tips close.

6. *Being rigid in the entire body.* Even though you're putting pressure on the skis to keep them apart in the V position, you can still maintain some flexing action in the ankle and knee joints (bob lightly up from the feet), and a more relaxed upper body (hold the poles with a looser grip, remember to take a few deep breaths before your start, and smile). You can't ski the snowplow if you're limp or stiff. The happy medium is to be poised but supple.

Ideal Terrain to Practice On

A long gentle slope that has packed snow.

Skating on Skis

What Is It?

When you skate on skis you take skating steps (a push-off from one ski and a glide on the other) while skiing downhill or across level ground.

Why Learn It?

Skating on skis is useful as a maneuver and is also one of the most profitable exercises a beginner can practice:

1. You'll use the skating step when getting off tows and lifts.

2. It enables you to increase your speed. This is particularly practical when you have a long and relatively shallow area to cross. Without skating, you will spend more time and energy walking.

3. Skating on skis is an excellent exercise. It teaches you to make a complete shift of weight with each step to balance and glide on one ski, to control your edges as you edge to push off but glide on a flat ski; and finally, it permits you to have the fun and gracefulness of setting up a rhythm.

4. Because it involves picking your skis (one at a time) off the snow, it helps you become accustomed to their weight and feel. For that reason, it is an ideal exercise to use as a warm-up on your first run in the morning.

5. By the time you reach advanced skiing, you will find it is a good way to change direction when skiing downhill, particularly in broken, chunky snow,

where you are not sure you can turn the skis smoothly on the surface of the snow.

How to Do It

Find a long but very, very gradual hill. Start to ski straight down the hill. While you are moving slowly down the fall line in your normal running position, pick up your left ski and angle the front of it out to the left side. Push your body (with flexed knee) onto the left ski in a gliding movement, by pushing off from the right ski. Lower your body slightly by bending the left knee and ankle further forward. Now start to rise and push off at the same time, pushing your body onto the right ski, which you have brought forward and angled out to the right. Glide a moment on the right ski. Toward the end of the glide, bring your left ski forward and angle it off to the left side. Push from the right ski into the left, leaning toward it from the waist. In order to push against the ski, you must force the inside edge into the snow. Press that knee inward and then press against the edge on the up motion. Glide onto a flat ski. Ride it until your momentum expires. Then edge it and push off onto the opposite ski (held flat). Let your arms swing with a little exaggeration to help you balance. Make believe your skis have become ice skates and you're skating in a rink.

Skate down again, this time concentrating on setting up a rhythm, letting your upper body swing forward from one step-glide to the next. See if you can generate some power in your leg thrust and then a smooth glide.

During your first few skating runs, carry your poles off the ground. After you begin to get the knack, you can use your poles to help your leg thrust. As in walking, you'll be thrusting with the right leg and the left pole and then the left leg and the right pole.

After you have practiced skating down the gradual slope 5 or 6 times, do this exercise. It will strengthen your push-off movement. Go to a wide open level area where you can skate in a very wide circle. Make a series of skating steps to one side only, always pushing from one ski and gliding off onto the other. Skate in a big circle to the left. Lower your body by bending the right knee and ankle further forward. As you rise, push off the right ski into the left, which you have angled forward and to the left. Glide a moment on the left with your body directly over the left ski. (Your head should be directly over the left foot.) Bring the right ski alongside. Put your weight on it as you lower your body. As you rise, take another skating step to the left. The action becomes: skate to the left, bring the right ski alongside, skate to the left, together, skate to the left, together. Because you are on a flat surface you don't have the gravity of a slope to help, so you must generate the momentum with your push-off leg thrust. To maintain the momentum, bring up your outside ski and make the next push-off before the previous one has stopped completely.

Now skate in a circle to the right. All of the skating steps will be to the right; the leg thrusts from the left. Start by angling the right ski forward and to the right as you thrust from the left ski (edged on the inside). Glide onto the right ski. Quickly bring up the left, ready for the next thrusting. Skate to the right, bring up the left; skate to the right, bring up the left. Continue until you have skated in a complete circle.

Having practiced skating in a circle in each direction, skate directly across a level area. Once again, you won't have the downhill force of a hill to give you momentum. You can pick up speed by sinking low just before the thrust, and pushing off from the compressed position. Push from the left ski and glide onto the right. Then push from the right and glide onto the left. See how few skating steps you can take and still cross the entire area. This will get you to glide for the maximum distance with each skating step.

Common Mistakes and How to Avoid Them

1. *Not shifting your entire weight to the forward ski.* This is what is happening if you find yourself centered between the skis, taking a lot of quick steps without being able to glide on any of them. You should be centered directly over the forward ski. As the glide nears the finishing point, thrust your head and shoulders directly over the new gliding ski. When you push off onto the new skating step some forward lean makes it easier to shift your weight.

2. *Not edging the ski you're thrusting against.* If the ski is flat, you won't have firm contact with the snow to push against. It will skid away from you when you push back against it. To get firm contact with the snow for thrusting, press your knee inward as you come up out of the compressed leg position. Leaning forward as you thrust also helps force your inside edge against the snow.

3. *Bringing the left arm forward when you skate onto the left ski, and the right arm forward when you skate onto the right ski.* You should be using the opposite-arm-to-leg action, which will help you thrust. Did you ever see speed skaters on ice? They use the arms in almost a pumping motion. Skating on skis is somewhat similar, but because you are carrying poles, it is a little less vigorous. Your opposite arm coming forward will give you added power in your push-off and greater balance in the glide.

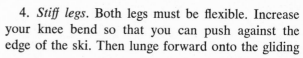

4. *Stiff legs.* Both legs must be flexible. Increase your knee bend so that you can push against the edge of the ski. Then lunge forward onto the gliding

Sequence in skating.

ski with the bent knee so that you can ride it in a balanced position directly over the ski.

5. *Practicing on a slope that's too steep*. When you've reached the advanced stage, you'll enjoy skating down moderately steep slopes. It's fun. But we don't recommend it when you're just learning how. You'll probably pick up too much speed when you first start in your downhill running position and then not be able to sink, edge, thrust, and glide. Make it easy for yourself. Try it first on the gentlest slope you can find.

6. *Lifting the back of the gliding ski higher than the tip when pushing off onto it*. You can easily catch the tip in the snow and spill. Be sure to lift the tip higher than the back and it will always clear the snow when you bring it forward.

Ideal Terrain to Practice On
A long but very gradual slope.

Skating in a circle.

Chapter Eight

RIDING TOWS AND LIFTS

IN THE EARLY STAGES of learning to ski, climbing is one of the most useful parts of your training. It strengthens the leg muscles, increases stamina, and it gives you practice in edging as well as a better feel of the skis while you are getting accustomed to their weight and length. But even more important, climbing allows you to use small slopes that may not be serviced by lifts or tows, or the bottom parts of larger slopes.

But climbing has its limitations. It consumes valuable time that could be spent skiing down the slope. It also is energy-consuming. If you climb too far or too many times within a short period, you won't have any energy left for practice.

At most ski areas there are gentle beginners' slopes which are serviced by tows or lifts. Now that you can turn to both sides and stop (by continuing your turn until you're turning back up the hill), you can make maximum use of your energy and time by learning to ride the lifts.

Before you ride a tow or lift be sure there is a way down suitable for someone with your ability! Nothing will destroy your confidence more quickly (and hinder your progress besides) than for you to arrive at the top of the lift and find that there are only intermediate or expert slopes and trails open to you. These are steeper, narrower, bumpier, and more winding than you can safely ski down with only limited experience in the snowplow. If by chance this does happen, ride the lift back down again, if possible. If not, take off your skis and walk down. Ask the lift attendant or ski patrolman for the best way down and stay out of the middle of the slope. If you don't, you're liable to get hit by other skiers on their way down. You'll also leave foot holes in

the snow, which are safety hazards to the other skiers.

There are three main types of lifts and tows. First is the kind that lets you stand on your skis on the snow and pulls you up the hill. Rope tows, J-bars, T-bars, and Poma lifts (or platter pulls) are in this category. When riding the second type, you keep your skis on while the conveyance lifts you off the ground and carries you uphill. Single, double, and side-riding chair lifts belong in this group. The third major type of lift, which is becoming more popular, rides you to the top without your skis on. Cable cars, gondola lifts ("bubble" lifts), and skimobiles are examples of this category.

Whenever you're going to ride a lift you have never been on before, ask the area attendants or ski patrol how to ride it—how to get on and how it unloads. It may be different from others that seem to be the same.

Tows That Pull You Uphill

ROPE TOW

The rope tow consists of a long continuous rope that goes around one wheel or pulley at the top of the hill and another at the bottom. The rope moves at a constant speed. It isn't difficult to use if you remember these pointers: The rope pulls you uphill while you're standing, so don't try to sit or squat. When you are next in line to use the tow, step out to the starting area. Get your skis into a parallel position, pointing directly up the tow line. If there are already grooves worn into the snow, start with your skis in the grooves. Hang both poles from their straps on the wrist of the hand furthest away from

(Opposite) Riding a rope tow.

1

2

3

4

5

6

the rope. Be sure you tuck into your parka or ski pants all loose clothing (such as scarves, long mufflers, shirt tails, etc.) which might catch and become entangled with the rope.

The object is to avoid getting jerked off your feet. Two things will help you minimize the starting jolt. Using the hand closest to the rope, hold the rope loosely so that it slips through your palm. Then gradually tighten your grip around the rope. At the same time lean back slightly and walk a few steps. By the time you've fully tightened your grip on the rope you're already in motion and your skis are sliding on the snow. When riding any of the lifts in this category, you can reduce the starting jolt by walking with the lift as you get on. Here's why this works. If the lift is moving at 8 miles an hour and you are standing motionless, the difference between its speed and yours is the full 8 miles per hour. If you start to walk at 3 miles an hour, when you get on the tow, you've reduced the difference to 5 miles per hour.

You have gradually grasped the rope with your hand nearest to it. Once you have started to move uphill, grab the rope just behind your back with the other hand. The ski poles will be hanging behind you from the wrist of that hand. Continue to ride in a standing position, leaning slightly back so that your feet are in front of your body. Don't squat or try to sit. Stand with your ankles and knees flexed to absorb the bumps and unevenness in the tracks.

Be sure to wear gloves or mittens with sturdy palms—either leather or reinforced fabric. The friction of the rope against your grip will quickly wear through unprotected wool. In the spring, wear the outside shell gloves to protect your hands.

When you are within 5 yards of the unloading area at the top let go with the hand behind you. Be sure your poles are clear of the rope. Then, when you get to the exact place where you want to get off, let go with the front hand. Step the outside ski off to the side with a skating step. Quickly move out of the way of the other skiers following you on the tow.

These are the important things to remember: Start with your skis parallel, pointing directly up the lift line; squeeze the rope gradually; walk with it as you tighten your grip; stand, leaning back; absorb the bumps and ruts in your ankles and knees; and keep the poles behind you.

J-BAR

The J-bar is composed of a series of wooden or metal J-shaped bars attached to a continuously moving cable. You ride uphill by standing and leaning back against the crook of the J-bar. Riding a J-bar is similar to riding a rope tow, but it's easier. Instead of holding on and being pulled up by your hands and arms, you lean back against it while it pulls you up by the seat. Use the same method to get on the J-bar as for the rope tow. Stand in the loading area with your skis parallel, pointing directly up the lift line. Hang both poles from the wrist furthest away from the lift. When the J-bar approaches you from the rear, turn from the waist and reach back with your free hand grabbing the upright part of the bar. Bring the horizontal or curved part underneath your seat and lean back against it.

Usually there is a lift attendant to let you get the horizontal part of the bar properly set against your body, just below your derrière. Walk a few shuffling steps with the J-bar to minimize the initial jolt, and then just stand and lean back against it. Don't try to sit on it. You'll end up being lifted into the air if the supporting towers are high, or else you'll pull the bar down to the ground with you. Hold the horizontal bar with your free hand (the one nearest the upright); hold the end of the J-bar with the other hand. Your poles will trail behind you, off to the side of your skis.

When you arrive at the unloading area at the top, push yourself forward and to the side away from the J-bar, pushing against the bar itself to get leverage. Lift the outside ski up and out of the track. Put your weight on this ski in a step-gliding movement. Then quickly take a few steps out of the way of the next skiers coming up the lift. Watch out for the returning J-bars! You may be hit if you don't watch their movement carefully.

T-BAR

This type of lift is a continuous, moving cable with upside-down T-bars attached to the cable. There is usually some sort of springing or hydraulic device between the T-bar and the main cable. This enables each individual T-bar to move closer to, or further from, the moving cable, thereby making it easier for the skiers to ride up over varied and uneven terrain. The T-bar is capable of pulling two skiers on each T, one on each side of the horizontal piece.

The principles of riding it are the same as those used in riding a J-bar, with only minor differences in the technique of getting on and off. Stand with your skis parallel, pointing directly up the lift line. Both poles hang from the wrist of the outside hand, away from the vertical bar. As the T-bar approaches, turn from the waist, toward the other person riding the lift with you, and reach back with your free (inside) hand. Grab the upright bar as it comes up to you. Look forward. Take a few shuffling steps to

1   2

3   4

Getting off a T-bar.

5

minimize the starting jolt. The attendant will delay the forward motion of the bar and will place it against your body, just beneath your seat. Now all you have to do is lean back against the bar and let it pull you up the hill. Ride in an erect position with your weight on both skis, ankles and knees loose. Generally, when you arrive at the top, the person riding on the outside track will get off first, by pushing forward and away from the T-bar. He moves off to the side. Push away from the T-bar with the inside hand by pushing against the upright bar near the cross piece. At the same time, lift the outside ski out of the track and take a skating step on it. You can then lift the inside ski out of the track and move out of the way. Watch out for the

T-bars returning downhill. Be sure you're clear of their path. The second skier starts to get off as soon as the first has unloaded. If the unloading spot is not level, use the herringbone position (tails close together, tips spread apart, inside edges pressed into the snow) to prevent slipping backward as you get off.

Until you have ridden the T-bar many times, avoid going up with someone who is much taller or much smaller than you. The difference in your height or weight can lead to problems if you're not used to riding the T-bar.

POMA LIFT (OR PLATTER PULL)

The Poma lift uses a continuously moving cable. At the bottom are J-sticks that are not permanently fastened to the main cable. They can be attached to the moving cable by a lift attendant when the skier is ready. The Poma lift J-stick has a shorter curved piece than the conventional J-bar lift and a round disk (usually about 8 inches in diameter) is attached to the very end of the J. You ride uphill straddling the stick so that the disk or platter pulls you from behind the thighs. Stand, and lean back against the disk, keeping it behind you by pressing your thighs together and holding the bar in front of you with both hands. Be sure that your skis are parallel, and that the tips point up the lift line. Hang both poles around one wrist. When you are about to get on the lift the attendant will hand you a bar. Push it between your legs from the front, putting the disk behind the upper part of your thighs. Hold the bar firmly with both hands in front of your chest. Shuffle your skis back and forth to unstick them. When you tell the attendant you're ready, he will pull a lever which connects your stick to the moving cable. When you see him pull, start walking so that you are in motion when your bar becomes attached.

Riding the Poma is exactly like riding a J-bar or a T-bar. You stand erect with flexed knees and ankles, leaning back slightly to keep the feet ahead of the body. To get off, slide your hands down toward the bottom of the bar. Spread your legs apart and bring the disk and bar out in front of you. Lift your outside ski from the track as you let go of the bar. Skate off to the side.

Tows That Lift You to the Top

SINGLE CHAIR LIFT

The chair lift is more comfortable than any of the lifts in the first category. You can sit down and relax your legs all the way up. The individual chairs are permanently attached to and are suspended from the continuously moving cable. To get

on, move out to the designated place (sometimes a piece of painted wood embedded in the snow) and stand with your skis parallel, pointing directly up the lift line. Hold both poles in your outside hand, and as the chair approaches you from the rear, turn from the waist and reach back with your inside hand to grasp the chair. As it moves forward and touches your legs, sit down in it. An attendant will delay the motion of the chair and will help you into it. Most chair lifts have a safety bar which you can close across your lap. Usually you have to lift the safety bar and then swing it across. Sometimes there is also a foot rest bar connected to the safety bar which swings into position at the same time. You can lift your skis onto it and rest your leg muscles. Read the instruction signs on the towers. They'll keep you informed of the things you need to know about mid-station unloading, if there is any; distance to the summit, and brief hints on when and how to unload. If there is a mid-station unloading platform and you intend to continue on to the summit, make sure your ski tips and poles are clear of the platform as you pass over it.

There are two common unloading situations: One in which there is a small ramp directly ahead and you ski down it to unload; and the other where the area is level and you ski off to the side of the moving chairs. In both cases you have to prepare to unload by lifting the safety bar and swinging it open. Move a bit forward in the chair so that you're ready to stand on your skis. Be sure to keep your ski tips

Loading onto a chair lift.

raised as you approach the unloading station. Otherwise they might catch in the snow or ramp and flip you out of the chair. When you get to the exact spot for unloading, *stand up on both skis*. If there is a ramp directly ahead to lead you out of the way of the moving chairs, ski down it in your normal running position and make a snowplow turn to stop. If the unloading spot is just a level area, *stand up on both skis and push yourself forward and off to the side of the chair*. Push against the chair itself with your free hand to get leverage and skate out of the way.

DOUBLE CHAIR LIFT

Double chair lifts take two skiers at a time. In some cases, there are actually two individual chairs attached to the same suspension bar, one on each side. On other lifts, the chair is one wide bench seat. The technique for getting on is the same as that for a single chair lift. Getting off may be different because two of you will be stepping out at the same time. In most cases, each skier gets off on his own side, *standing up on both skis and pushing himself forward and away from the chair with his free hand.*

Sometimes the unloading area is set up so that after getting off, one skier must wait until the chair has passed by. Then he can move across the track to the opposite side where the warming hut and slopes are located. Watch out for the moving chairs going in both directions. Once off the chair, move out of the way of the next skiers unloading.

Cars That Take You to the Top

Cable cars (in which a dozen or more skiers may stand), gondola cars which look like bubble cars (in which two or three skiers sit) skimobiles (in which one or two skiers stand) are a few of the kinds of lifts that carry skiers who are not wearing their skis. Usually they are enclosed and are the warmest of the three basic kinds of lifts. Almost always you are loaded into, and unloaded from, a stationary car, so you have no problem getting in or out. If your skis are to ride in the rack outside the car it's a good idea to fasten them together. In any case, follow the basic rule: If you haven't taken that particular lift before ask how it loads and unloads before you get on it.

Chapter Nine

BUILDING TOWARD ADVANCED SKIING

YOU'VE COMPLETED the first phase of learning to ski. You can walk and get around on level ground. You can climb up small hills, and ski down gentle slopes, linking turns in the snowplow position. Now you're ready to start building toward more advanced skiing when you will ultimately ski with your legs close together and your skis parallel. This way of skiing is the most graceful, most effortless, most controlled, and most fun.

You have learned valuable lessons which you will continue to use. For example, you have had practice in edging your skis, in shifting your weight from one ski over to the other, in leaning out over your outside boot, and in bobbing lightly from your feet so that your ankles and knees are supple. You'll use each one of these movements during your entire ski life. However, you have been doing them in the somewhat awkward snowplow position which you learned so that you'd have an almost immediate means of turning and braking. Now you'll be doing these things while your legs are together part of the time. Eventually, you'll be skiing with them together all the time.

The difference between your old stance and your new one (legs close together and skis parallel) may seem relatively insignificant. Actually it's much more than a minor change in your position. When you learn to ski with your body directly over both legs, you'll find it less tiring than skiing the snowplow. You'll be able to ski for longer periods, with greater control, and at higher speeds, if you so desire. And you'll be able to negotiate narrower, steeper, and more difficult slopes and trails.

The first step in the process is to learn to ski across the slope with your legs in a close compact position. This is called "traversing."

Traversing

What Is It?

Traversing is skiing diagonally down a slope, for which you'll use a special traversing position. Any time you're skiing in a straight line without skiing directly down the fall line, you're traversing.

Why Learn It?

It enables you to ski diagonally down and across the hill in a balanced position with your legs close together and your skis parallel. *Traversing* is the basic position from which you'll start and finish the advanced turns you'll be learning. You'll use it to get down slopes when the snow conditions or the terrain of a slope make it difficult or unwise to make more than the minimum number of turns. Between these few turns you'll be making long traverses.

How to Do It

Begin to practice this position by traversing across the hill in a very shallow descent. That is, ski a line that takes you across, but only a small distance lower, on the hill. Start from the side of the slope so that you can take full advantage of its width. Stand erect with your legs close together and your skis parallel. Advance your uphill ski about 4 inches and with it your uphill knee, hip, and shoulder. Push your knees forward of your ankles. Bend sideways slightly at the waist so that your head is out over the lower boot and your upper body is leaning slightly downhill. In order for you to ski in a straight line your uphill edges will have to be angled into the snow. Roll your knees into the hill and your edges will bite. To balance this sideways bend in your legs, lean away from the hill with your head and shoul-

Traversing position.

ders. Both poles will be pointing across the skis into the hill. In this position, your weight is on the lower ski while the uphill ski rides almost unweighted out ahead. From the front view, your body position describes a large comma.

Some instructors have had success in teaching the traverse position by telling their pupils to plug their hips into the hill. Others describe the position by saying, "Turn your back uphill." Here's another way of thinking of it. You're wearing a diamond studded belt buckle. On every traverse you turn your hips to show the belt buckle to the people on the hill below you. All of these phrases refer to the same characteristics of traverse position: *uphill* ski, knee, hip, and shoulder are advanced; then the knees and hips are pressed into the hill while the upper body leans away from the hill; the head, shoulders, and hips are turned to face further downhill than the direction of the skis, with the downhill shoulder drawn back and slightly lowered. The result is that *most of your weight will be on the downhill ski and your uphill edges will be biting into the snow.* With your boots and knees touching each other you should feel that this position is compact.

Try this little experiment and you'll feel the "hips in–lean out" aspect of the traverse position. Ask someone to help you. It will only take a few seconds. Stand on a slope with your skis across the fall line. Have your helper stand down the hill 4 feet below the front end of your skis. Ask him to hold the baskets of your poles and try to pull the poles away from him. If he resists and even tugs a little, you'll find your upper body is drawn downhill while your hips and knees are pushing into the hill to keep your balance. There you are!

Ski across the width of the slope in this traverse position, bobbing up and down lightly (perhaps an inch or 2 at most) from the feet. When you get to within 5 or 6 yards of the far side, while you're still in motion, take a few steps up the hill, starting with your uphill ski. Lift it off the snow and point the tip farther uphill. Step all your weight onto that ski. Bring the lower ski up alongside it. Pushing off the lower ski, step the upper ski tip further uphill, etc. You'll come to a stop as the fronts of the skis face uphill. Look back at your traversing tracks. You should be able to see two parallel lines where your edges bit into the snow. Get into the traverse posi-

Tugging experiment to feel "hips in—lean out."

tion facing the opposite direction and ski across the width of the slope, again picking a line that is not steep. As you approach the far side, take small skating steps uphill, changing the direction of the fronts of the skis until you stop.

Practice your traverse position to both directions picking a slightly steeper line across the same hill after each few traverses. *Practice the traverse position until you feel familiar and somewhat comfortable skiing that way. You'll be skiing in variations of this position a great part of the time. Be sure you have mastered it.*

Common Mistakes and How to Avoid Them

1. *Leaning your head and shoulders into the hill.* This brings your weight onto the uphill ski and usually ends in a sit-down fall into the hill. There are several ways which will remind you to carry your weight on the outside or downhill ski. Traverse the slope lifting the back of your inside (uphill) ski 4 or 5 inches off the snow. This forces you to put your weight over the downhill ski. A second exercise is to traverse pretending a friend is below you on the hill and has engaged you in a small tug of war with

your poles. A third exercise is to ski across in traverse position and as you go, reach down and touch the outside of your downhill leg just above the top of your boot.

2. *Uphill ski not in front of the downhill ski.* The uphill ski will invariably run on top of the front part of your downhill ski. The curvature of the tip of the downhill ski will prevent the uphill ski from crossing it if the uphill ski is beyond this curved part. Once the uphill ski falls behind the curved part, there is nothing to keep it from running across the flat part of the downhill ski. Correct this mistake by bending both knees toward the tips as you "open" the position of your hips (turn them so that your uphill hip is forward, your downhill hip back). Your uphill knee should be in front of your downhill knee.

3. *Uphill ski too far advanced.* There are at least two ways to tell when your uphill ski is too far ahead of your downhill ski. The first is if there is a big forward space (more than a few inches) between your boots. The second is if your shinbone isn't slanting backwards from the knee to the ankle. The further forward you push the uphill ski, the more difficult it is to maintain the desired knee-forward-

of-the-ankle position which insures ankle-bend. If the uphill ski is too far forward it tends to "hook" or turn uphill sometimes causing a spill. Correct this by keeping your boots touching each other.

4. *Traversing on flat skis.* When this happens, you lose your edge contact with the slope and your flat skis slide sideways toward the bottom of the hill. Force both knees, one against the other, into the hill. Look down at your skis and see how the edges are now set into the snow.

5. *Carrying your elbows pressed against your body with your hands at your chest.* Your arm muscles will tire quickly in this position, and your arms won't give you the necessary balance. Carry your arms about waist high, with your elbows 4 to 6 inches away from your body, poles pointing behind you.

Ideal Terrain to Practice On
A wide slope that is not steep.

Stemming—A Half Snowplow

What Is It?
Stemming is the action of stepping one ski into the V position, with the ski tips close, but not touching, and the tails spread apart. Since only one of the skis is in this position, it is called "the half snowplow."

Why Learn It?
Stemming is most useful as the beginning of several turning maneuvers. Because the stemmed ski is pointing in a new direction, as soon as you put weight on it you will have changed your direction. You'll use it as soon as you progress to the next section (combining long traverses with the snowplow turn). You will use it also when you learn the higher speed stem christie turn. In both of these turns you stem the uphill ski. However, stemming the lower ski can sometimes be useful as a braking movement. Because it uses muscle force of one leg to effect the braking, it should be used as sparingly as possible.

How to Do It
Try this movement on level ground first. Stand in the traverse position, as though you were traversing from the right to the left side of the hill. Step your uphill (left) ski into the V position, making sure your left knee is bent forward and the ski is edged. Simultaneously turn your head and shoulders to face out over the front of the left foot. Increase the bend in the right knee so that your body is lowered. Your weight remains on the downhill (right) ski throughout the movement. Your right arm comes up ready

to plant the right pole. Now return to your traverse position by raising your body (straightening out the right leg) and stepping the left ski close alongside your right. Your head and shoulders have returned to their position facing out over the right boot. Repeat this exercise 6 times or until you feel the coordination of stepping the ski, turning the head and shoulders, and lowering the body at the same time while the weight stays on the downhill ski. Then practice it in the traverse position to the other side, reversing the words "right" and "left" in the instruction.

Now you're ready to practice stemming while in motion, traversing the slope. Pick a hill that isn't steep, but that is wide enough so you can stem your uphill ski 5 or 6 times on each run. Start across the hill in a traverse. Your weight should be on the downhill ski. Using the movements you just practiced on level ground, step the uphill ski into the V position as you lower your body, and turn your head and shoulders out over the uphill foot. Hold that position for a few seconds, then return to your original traverse position. Repeat the stemming-and-returning-to-traverse as you continue across the hill. When you approach the far side of the slope, come to a stop by taking small skating steps up the hill in the same manner as when you were practicing traversing. Because your weight remains on the downhill ski during the entire time you're going across the hill, there should be no change in your direction. Become adept in stemming while traversing in both directions.

Common Mistakes and How to Avoid Them
1. *Starting from an incorrect traverse position.* If you don't have your weight on the lower ski with the uphill ski, knee, hip, and shoulder advanced when you begin this exercise, there is little chance you'll be able to arrive at the proper stem position. Review your traverse position and be certain it's correct before practicing this one.

2. *Stepping out the uphill ski parallel to the lower ski.* This is not a stem because the ski is not pointing in a new direction. When you step the ski out, keep the tips within a few inches of each other but spread the tails wide apart.

3. *Stepping out the uphill ski with too much edge.* The stemmed ski should skid in the V position. If you have angled the ski too far to the inside, it will run straight along the edge and cross your downhill ski. Correct this by moving your knee over the ski a little more so as to flatten it a bit.

4. *Failing to turn the head and shoulders over the boot of the stemmed ski.* Your upper body won't be

Sequence in stem exercise.

in the proper position for turning when you shift your weight to the uphill ski. Once the head and shoulders are positioned in stemming, they stay in that position throughout the turn with a minimum amount of movement. They have to be positioned properly at the beginning.

5. *Not lowering the body (by increasing the ankle- and knee-bend of the lower ski) when the uphill ski is stemmed*. This will cause problems when you learn to make stem christies. In that turn, you'll be using a down-up-forward-down action to make it easier to shift weight. The "down" part of that sequence is done while stemming.

Ideal Terrain to Practice On
A wide, moderately steep hill.

Stem Turn

What Is It?
A stem turn involves skiing down a hill using a long traverse, then going into a snowplow position to make the change of directions, and returning to a traverse in the new direction.

Why Learn It?
1. The combination of maneuvers, which you have already learned individually, enables you to ski down wide slopes with your skis parallel and your legs close together much of the time (whenever you're not in the process of turning). Previously, when you linked snowplow turns, your skis were in the V-position the entire time, never parallel.

2. You'll learn to start turns from the traverse position (the same body position from which you'll start all of your advanced turns).

3. You'll learn to start turns while skiing across the slope. This is different from starting turns while skiing down the fall line, as you did when learning the snowplow turn.

How to Do It
Traverse a slope that's wide but not steep, bobbing lightly from the feet to keep in motion and not in a static position. As you approach the far side, stem the uphill ski into a V-position (tips close, tails apart). At the same time lower your body (by increasing the forward bend in your downhill knee and ankle) and turn your head and shoulders toward the stemmed ski. At this moment you'll be in a half snowplow position facing uphill! Hold that upper

Sequence in stem turn.

body position and shift your weight over to (against) the stemmed ski. Your head should be directly above the little toe. You'll start to turn. In a few moments, as the turn continues into the fall line add more turning power by applying turning action of the legs. Pretend you're putting out a cigarette butt underneath the boot of your stemmed ski. As you turn across the fall line into the new direction, *the stemmed ski will become the downhill ski.* Your upper body position is relatively unchanged from the time you leaned out over the stemmed ski; and it's already in the proper position for the new traverse. Bring the inside ski into the new traverse position (close alongside but forward of the downhill ski) by raising your body up and forward, out of the snowplow and sliding or stepping the skis together.

Common Mistakes and How to Avoid Them

1. *See the mistakes and corrections described in the section on stemming.*

2. *Failing to return to the proper traverse position.* When you come out of the half snowplow, be sure that your inside (now uphill) ski is leading, that your outside (now downhill) shoulder is lowered and drawn back, and that your hips are turned slightly downhill.

Ideal Terrain to Practice On

A wide, moderately steep slope.

Chapter Ten

CHRISTIES–
CONTROLLED SKIDDING TURNS

"CHRISTIE" IS SHORT FOR "CHRISTIANIA" and refers to a type of advanced turn in which the skis are skidded around the middle and final part of the turn. That is, after you have started to turn the skis, they slip sideways as they continue to turn. The stem christie and parallel christie turns are your means of skiing at higher speeds and on more difficult slopes where the snowplow and stem turns are not suitable.

The crux of the christie turn is controlled edging. At the proper time the edges must be released sufficiently to allow the skis to skid sideways around the turn and then re-edged in the new traverse. The key to this control is side-slipping.

Side-Slipping

What Is It?
Side-slipping is the controlled flattening out of the skis to produce a sideways skidding. By releasing the pressure of the edges against the snow, the skis will slip. By applying progressively increasing pressure, your skidding will get slower and slower until you apply full edges with forceful pressure and come to a complete stop. You can control the *directions* of your side-slipping with the forward–backward position of your *weight,* and the *speed* of your skidding by the amount of knee pressure into the hill. Side-slipping is both an exercise in edge control and a useful maneuver in itself.

Why Learn It?
1. *Side-slipping* is the core of faster, more advanced turns in which the skis slide sideways over the snow.
2. You'll use side-slipping (now and when you

are an advanced skier as well) to get down slopes and trails that are too steep or too difficult for you to handle any other way. It is particularly useful in parts of trails that are too narrow for the turns you know and too steep for you to run straight. You can side-slip through the narrows.

How to Do It
Find a slope that has a short fairly steep pitch. The gravity pull will be moving you down the hill. If you try to learn side-slipping on a gradual hill you won't have enough gravitational force to help you.

You can side-slip in 3 directions: directly down the fall line, diagonally forward, and diagonally backward. Side-slipping directly down the fall line is used in negotiating narrow places. Side-slipping forward is closest to the feeling of skidding in a turn. Side-slipping backward can be useful in a trail and is also good practice for controlling your weight while in the traverse position. Learn the straight side-slip first.

Stand on the steep part of the hill in the traverse position, with your legs touching. They will be working as a unit and as such should be very close together. In order to remain stationary in that position, apply your edges against the snow.

Now, let's start. Stand in a traverse (comma) position, skis pointing across the hill to the left. Your uphill (left) ski is advanced about half a boot length while most of your weight is on the downhill (right) ski. Your uphill hip and shoulder are also forward; this position has the effect of turning your head, shoulders, and hips toward the bottom of the hill. You have a sideways break at the waist so that your

Side—slipping.

upper body is leaning out away from the hill. Your knees are pressed into the hill so that your edges are applied against the snow. Your aim now is to release your edges and slip sideways down the hill.

Put your uphill (left) pole in the snow above your skis, about a foot in front of your left boot. Place your lower pole in the snow about 2 feet below your skis, opposite the back end of your right boot. You're now standing between your poles, close to the upper one. To release the edges and initiate the sideways slipping, *straighten up in your knees and ankles and at the same time bring your knees away from the*

Side—slipping between your poles.

hill. This has the effect of "flattening out" the skis. When you have skidded down to your lower pole, push your knees into the hill again, re-establishing your edge bite and stopping your sliding motion.

Practice this straight side-slipping between your poles 8 or 10 times facing in each direction. If you have trouble getting slipping action started, try pushing yourself downhill from the upper pole. Remember, don't be discouraged if the first few times you try this it doesn't work perfectly. Side-slipping is one of the more difficult movements. But it's also one of the most important, so keep practicing until you get it.

This is the second exercise to practice. Start from the traverse position. Lift your poles off the snow as you release your edges (with a straightening-up motion) and bring your knees away from the hill. Side-slip straight down 3 or 4 yards, then apply your edges with enough knee pressure to stop. Release again, skid, and stop. Practice starting from a position facing in each direction. Then try this version: Make a mark in the snow with your pole. Then climb up 10 or 12 yards above the mark. Now, side-slip straight down at a slow even speed, stopping exactly at the mark.

The next series of exercises will help you get the knack of skidding the skis sideways and forward at the same time. Start by traversing in a shallow traverse (you're headed more across the hill than down it). Ski across part way, then rise up from your traverse position and bring your knees away from the

hill to flatten out the skis. You'll start to skid sideways as you continue forward. In effect, you'll be skidding diagonally down the hill. Continue to skid diagonally for the full width of the slope, stopping at the far side by pushing your knees into the hill vigorously. If you look back at your ski tracks in the snow you should see two straight lines where your skis were edged in the traverse, and then skid marks when you began side-slipping.

Throughout all these side-slipping exercises, you should be carrying more weight on the lower ski and your upper body should remain quiet. *The action is all in the legs.* Next try the forward side-slip starting from a traverse, and stopping every 15 feet or so by edging. After you have done this variation a half dozen times to each side, do the next one.

Start from a stationary traverse (comma) position. Release your edges and side-slip directly down the fall line a short way. Continue to skid as you bring your body weight slightly forward so that you've changed from a straight side-slip to a diagonal slip. Skid diagonally forward for a few yards, then stop by applying your edges forcefully into the hill. From your stationary position, side-slip directly down the hill again. Skid for a few yards. This time shift your weight slightly to the back of the skis as you're slipping. You should go into a backward diagonal side-slip.

The last of the side-slipping exercises is the zigzag. Start by going into a forward side-slip while you're moving across the hill in a traverse. Continue the

Skidding the skis forward and sideways simultaneously.

forward slip until you get to the far side. Apply your edges. Slow down almost to a complete stop, but not quite. Bring your weight back to its centered position so that you are slowly slipping straight down the fall line. Then shift your weight backwards and release your edges a little more so that you begin to side-slip diagonally backwards. Side-slip diagonally back and forth across the slope. This is not an easy exercise to perfect, but the time you spend practicing it will greatly reduce the time it takes to learn the stem christie and parallel christie turns.

Common Mistakes and How to Avoid Them

1. *Not starting from the proper traverse position.* It is absolutely essential that you start with your uphill ski, knee, hip, and shoulder all advanced, your legs touching each other, and most of your weight on the lower ski. Otherwise, you won't be able to stay balanced once the skis begin to skid. Check your traverse position carefully before you release your edges.

2. *Rolling your knees too far out, away from the hill.* Your skis will flatten out to a point where your downhill edges will catch on the slightest unevenness

in the terrain and you'll fall. Bring your knees away from the hill slowly. You'll find that you will skid sideways long before your skis are absolutely flat on the hill.

3. *Allowing your skis to separate.* The wider apart your skis, the tougher it is to control the edging. Usually, they separate when you put too much weight on the upper ski. Lean your upper body out over the lower ski. Then make a conscious effort to keep the upper knee and boot pressed into the lower knee and boot. Being positioned directly over both feet makes it much easier to control the edges of the skis.

4. *Leaning the upper body into the hill.* When you do flatten out the skis, they'll slide out from under you, causing an uphill fall. To remain balanced over the skis, you must continue to lean out from the waist. The edge control takes place in the action of the knees moving into and away from the hill.

5. *Uphill ski falling behind and across the lower ski.* As in the traversing position, the upturned front of the lower ski prevents the upper ski from crossing onto it only when the upper ski is in front of the

upturned part. Once the upper ski lags behind, it generally runs right across the lower ski, dumping you into the snow. Correct this by starting in the proper traverse position and maintaining the position by keeping *both knees bent forward as you lean out.* Your weight is distinctly on the downhill ski. The unweighted uphill ski rides slightly forward.

Ideal Terrain to Practice On
A short, steep slope that has a good snow covering.

Parallel Christie into the Hill

What Is It?
This is a skidded uphill turn (starting from a traverse in the same direction) in which your skis remain parallel throughout the turn.

Why Learn It?
1. It is the same movement as the last part of the stem christie and parallel christie turns. By practicing christies into the hill you'll learn quicker.

2. When the turn is executed sharply into the hill, it is an effective method of coming to a complete stop.

3. These are your first turns in which your skis remain parallel from start to finish.

How to Do It
Make your first christies into the hill gradual turns. Start in a shallow traverse (pointing your skis more across than down the hill). Traverse until you have some momentum. Lower your body just a bit. Then with an up motion (by straightening the ankles and knees) relax the edge pressure and allow the backs of the skis to start skidding sideways. Now, as you sink back into a position of increased knee- and ankle-bend *turn the skis uphill by turning the feet and knees into the hill.* Your upper body stays in its original traverse position, leaning out over the outside boot. Your weight remains on the lower ski throughout the entire turn.

Your objective is to start the skis skidding and then apply turning force to them, while you push your hips towards your boots. As in all maneuvers, learn to do this in both directions before trying the next one. Then practice making parallel christies into the hill from progressively steeper traverses. As your starting traverse line gets steeper and steeper, you will pick up more speed in the traverse. The trick is to start the turn before you are going so fast you can't concentrate on the movements. To avoid this,

ski a shorter distance in the traverse position, and then start the christie into the hill sooner than you did on previous practice runs. Also, as your starting traverse line gets steeper, your comma position will become more pronounced.

In each of these parallel christies into the hill, you must stay in the turn until the tips of your skis are pointing back uphill and you have come to a stop.

Common Mistakes and How to Avoid Them
1. *See the section on traversing. The mistakes described there are common to this maneuver.*

2. *Bringing the outside hip forward when beginning the turn.* The skier ends up with his weight on the uphill ski, leaning into the hill. The turning action should be a turning of the feet and knees. Hips and shoulders remain in the traverse position, with the downhill hip and shoulder drawn back.

3. *Sitting back.* This happens when you "sit in the chair"; your ankles are stiff, and excessive waist-bend pushes your hips back. The correction is basic to sitting back errors in all maneuvers. As you start the turning movement, thrust your hips forward so that they stay positioned directly above the feet, and do not drop back behind them. Your knees should be pushed forward of the ankles. The break at the waist is only a sideways bend.

4. *Not finishing with a down movement of the hips.* Although the down-up-down action is not pronounced in this maneuver, it is part of it. Complete your parallel christie into the hill by lowering your hips toward the front of your feet and turning the skis with your legs.

Ideal Terrain to Practice On
Any wide smooth slope of moderate steepness, but preferably one with a convex contour.

Christie-into-the-Hill Scallop

What Is It?
This is an exercise in which you make a number of christies into the hill on a single traverse across the slope.

Why Learn It?
1. You will be making an increased number of turns on each traverse thereby accelerating your learning process.

2. It will help you get used to the feeling of coming back into the fall line.

3. You'll learn the coordination of closing the skis

into the traverse position, increasing the ankle- and knee-bend as you apply turning action of the legs.

How to Do It

Start in a traverse across the slope. Make a christie into the hill in the same manner you have been practicing, but don't come to a complete stop. As your momentum starts to slow up near the end of your turn, step the uphill ski into a small stem position. Put a little weight on the stemmed ski so that your tips start to turn downhill. Once the skis are turning toward the fall line *push off against the stemmed ski,* putting your weight on the lower (outside) ski and bringing the stemmed ski back into the traverse position. From this traverse position you make another christie into the hill. Continue to stem the uphill ski to bring your skis almost into the fall line, and make christies into the hill away from the fall line. The lower ski carries most of your weight throughout the exercise and the upper body stays in the traverse position (downhill shoulder held back, sideways break at the waist).

Common Mistakes and How to Avoid Them

1. *Not starting from the proper traverse position.* This is one of the 3 mistakes most commonly retarding the progress of skiers to advance levels. To make christie turns, you must begin from the proper position. Check before you start your traverse position moving and maintain it as you traverse. If you find you're having trouble holding the proper position, go back and practice the traverse by itself. You'll derive more benefit from the time you spend mastering the traverse than from attempting to learn the skidding turns without being adept at traversing.

2. *Refer to the mistakes commonly made when christieing into the hill.*

3. *Not closing the skis quickly enough from the stem position.* The purpose of the small stem at the end of each christie into the hill is to change your direction toward the fall line so that you can make another turn uphill. You should have your skis close together and parallel as much of the time as possible. Don't linger in the stemmed position. Step the ski alongside the downhill ski quickly.

Ideal Terrain to Practice On

A wide, moderately steep hill.

Basic Pole Action in Christie Turns

Not so many years ago, skiers pushed their poles into the snow only to propel themselves along level ground or to push against when climbing. When they skied down, they carried their poles for balance but not for anything more. In today's skiing, proper pole action is important to all advanced turns; for on every stem christie, parallel christie, and wedeln turn the modern skier places his pole into the snow.

What Is It?

Pole action in christie turns involves placing the inside pole (left pole on turns to the left; right pole on turns to the right) into the snow at the moment your up motion unweights the skis.

Why Learn It?

1. As you momentarily press down on it, the pole helps transfer your weight from the inside to the outside ski.

2. Placing the pole properly into the snow helps position your upper body for the turn and for the coming traverse position.

3. The planted pole acts as a pivot around which the turning action of your skis takes place.

4. The action of planting and withdrawing the pole is an integral part of your timing and rhythm in all of the christie turns.

How to Do It

There is a basic pole action you should learn now. However, there is no one exact position in which to place the pole and no one degree of firmness to use in planting it for all turns at all times. You'll vary these factors to adjust for your speed, the condition of the snow, the terrain, and the kind of turn you're making. The variations that apply to each individual turn are discussed in those sections.

Here is the basic pole action and the timing: Stand in your straight running position on level ground when you first try this. Sink a little lower into your knees and ankles (in the same manner you lower your body when stemming). Now place your left pole into the snow about halfway between your boot and your left ski tip. Keep your elbow down and close to the body. The basket of the pole should be only a few inches to the left of the ski. Raise your body and remove the pole from the snow. The timing is down-pole-up. After you have lowered your body, the placing of the pole triggers the up movement.

Now pretend you're making a turn to the right. Increase the bend in your knees and ankles. Place the right pole into the snow about halfway to the right ski tip and a few inches away from the ski. Keep your elbow down. Come up and withdraw the pole at the same time. Do this exercise alternating

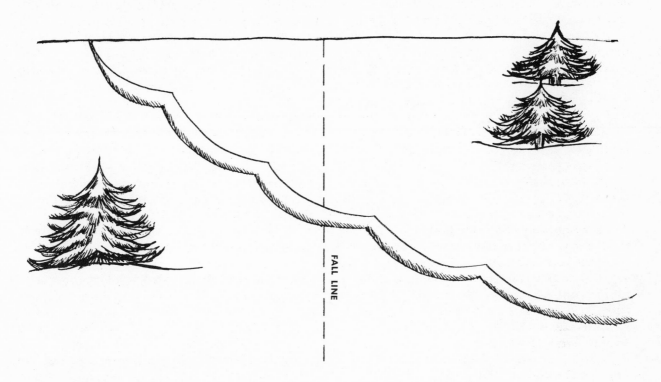

Tracks of skis—christie into the hill scallops.

the poles in a slow rhythm. Down-pole-up, down-pole-up, down-pole-up. Find a very gentle slope that has a long outrun. Try the same exercise while skiing down the fall line. There are no turns involved—simply the experience of planting the poles with the proper timing as you're moving down a hill.

There are two other pole action exercises you'll find useful later on. Do them on level ground only. In the first exercise pretend you're going to make a stem christie turn to the left. From your running position, stem the right ski into the V-position, lowering your body as you do it. Plant your left pole into the snow, close to the shovel (the forward part) of your left ski. Raise your body again, pushing down on the pole and as you come up. Step your left ski alongside your right ski. Finish by sinking down into your running position and removing the pole. This is the weight-transferring action you'll use in making stem christies! Add to this the skidding and the turning action of the legs, and you have the essentials of the stem christie turn.

The second pole action exercise will help you when you learn parallel hop christie turns. Here's what you're trying to do in this exercise. Pretend you are standing on a hill in a straight running position, pointing slightly left of the fall line. Bend ankles and knees forward, keeping your upper body erect. Sink lower into your legs (by increasing the ankle- and

knee-bend, but keeping the waist straight). Plant the right pole into the snow about 1 or 1½ feet forward of your right boot, close to the ski. Putting pressure on the pole momentarily, hop up very slightly and swing both ski tails to the left. The trick is to move the ski tails laterally rather than high off the ground. Land lightly by absorbing the impact in your ankles and knees. Allow your body to continue moving downward after your skis have made contact with the snow. Now flex both knees again. Plant the left pole keeping your elbow down. Lean on the pole for a split second and hop both ski tails across the line to the right. Finish by shoving your knees forward toward the front of the skis.

Here's a clue for adding gentleness to your hop. Use the same push from the balls of the feet as for jumping rope. The springing action is all in the legs, not a pumping motion of the trunk hinged at the belt line.

Do this down-pole-hop-down exercise in a series of 6 hops. Remember, always plant the pole on one side and hop the tails to the other side. This simulates the coordination you'll use in hop christies where you plant the pole on the inside of the turn you're about to make and then hop the tails to the outside of the turn. As a matter of fact, this holds true for all christie turns. Plant the pole on the inside and shift your weight to the outside. Remember to

keep your elbows fairly close to your body when planting the pole.

Common Mistakes and How to Avoid Them

1. *Putting the pole into the snow too far forward.* If you reach forward by bending at the waist, you're planting the pole too far forward. It should be put into the snow about 1 to 1½ feet in front of your boots. As you learn to ski with speed, you'll learn to place the pole properly, nearer the tip of the ski. The general rule is this. When you are skiing slowly, plant the pole closer to the boot and with more firmness. When you are skiing faster, place the pole further forward and with a lighter touch.

2. *Leaving the pole in the snow too long.* This will cause your inside arm and shoulder to lag behind, pulling your weight to the back part of your skis. When you're skiing down a hill, you should withdraw the pole while your hand and arm are still positioned in front of your body. Many instructors have found the following little device helpful to skiers learning pole action. After you have placed the pole into the snow, roll the palm of your wrist forward as you withdraw your pole. Instead of lifting the pole

Sequence of movement: basic pole action.

directly upward, lift forward and up at the same time.

3. *Placing the pole in the snow too far back.* This has the same effect as leaving it in the snow too long. When you are in motion skiing downhill, you will ski past the pole, which will pull your weight back and inside.

Ideal Terrain to Practice On

Level area at first, then a long gentle slope.

Stop Christie

What Is It?

A stop christie is a sharp skidding turn into the hill made with abrupt pressure on the uphill edges. The combination of the forceful turning action and the abrupt pressure on the edges brings you to a complete stop.

Why Learn It?

It's a quick, practical method of coming to a halt when you're skiing at moderate or high speed.

How to Do It

A stop christie is really a parallel christie into the hill that ends abruptly with a short sharp increase in edging, followed by a planting of the downhill pole.

The usual procedure of learning (by starting from a gradual traverse and then increasing the steepness of the starting direction on successive runs) has to be altered somewhat for this maneuver. It's actually more difficult to make a stop christie from a very shallow traverse than from a medium or steep traverse. You can't generate enough turning action.

So, on a short but moderately steep hill, traverse in a line about halfway between going straight down and going directly across. In the comma position, traverse far enough to pick up good momentum. Then sink slightly in the knees and ankles, and touch the uphill pole into the snow. With an up-forward movement in the legs, start the skis skidding sideways. Lower your hips toward the front of your boots and at the same time turn the skis with your legs. Push the ski tails out and your knees inward. Finish this sinking action with an abrupt drop against an increased edge angle. You get this by forcefully pressing your knees into the hill with a sharp movement. Then reach downhill with the outside arm and jab the downhill pole into the snow with the tip in front of your boot, your hand opposite your hip. This is often referred to as "dotting the i." It has the

Sequence of movement: stop christie.

effect of keeping you balanced over the skis. The sharp turn uphill and abrupt edging has a tendency to leave you leaning into the hill with your upper body. "Dotting the i" reminds you to break sideways at the waist downhill—to increase your weight on the downhill ski. It also gives a finishing movement to the stop.

Practice the stop christie from a traverse in both directions. Then practice it from progressively steeper starting traverses. Try to use the stop christie as your method of stopping. It's quick and it's a turn in which your skis remain parallel throughout the entire turn. That's a good habit for you to acquire. It is one of the single most useful maneuvers you can learn, so practice it at every opportunity.

Common Mistakes and How to Avoid Them

1. *Not enough turning action.* Basically, a stop christie is a sharp turn uphill. The abrupt drop and increased edging are the final part that follow the skidding part of the turn. To make this a sharp turn, concentrate on the second part of the turn (after you have unweighted the skis and started them sliding sideways). As you come into the final down phase of the down-up-down sequence, thrust your ski tails out and press your knees inward. This leg rotation will produce the turning action you need.

2. *Not making a sharp, decisive drop.* The movement which makes the stop christie effective (and different from an ordinary parallel christie into the hill) is the sudden forceful pressure against the uphill edges. This is not a gradual increase in pressure but rather a rapid one. You accomplish it by abruptly dropping and pushing your hips towards your boots.

3. *Leaning the upper body into the hill.* The sharper the turn you make, the greater the need for sideways bend at the waist to keep your weight on the lower ski. You automatically increase your comma position when you jab your outside pole into the snow as the final gesture of the turn.

4. *Not increasing your edge bite.* The sharp drop of your hips puts added pressure against your skis. But if the skis are flat on the snow, this pressure will have no braking effect. The pressure has to be applied against the edges, which cut into the snow. The key is to make the dropping and the increased edging a single movement. Push your hips down at the same time you force your knees into the hill.

Ideal Terrain to Practice On

A short steep hill.

Stem Christie Off the Fall Line

What Is It?

A stem christie off the fall line is an exercise in which you make a christie into the hill starting from a small or narrow snowplow directly down the fall line.

Why Learn It?

It simulates the movements of the middle and last part of a stem christie turn. Perhaps a better way to think of it is that you're making a stem christie, starting from the middle of the turn.

How to Do It

On a moderately steep but short hill, get into the ready position with your skis in a small snowplow pointing directly down the fall line. Before you start, *relax* a little. Loosen your death grip on the poles, flex your ankles and knees once or twice, take a deep breath, and *smile.* Ski straight down the fall line for about 6 or 8 feet, far enough to give you some momentum. Lower your body a few inches as you place the left pole into the snow approximately a foot ahead of your left boot. In one continuous movement, spring lightly up and forward (using the left pole for momentary support). Then shift your weight to the right ski, stepping the left ski alongside and slightly ahead of it. Break sideways at the waist, leaning out over the right ski. You should be in the traverse position. Finish the turn by using the same leg-turning action as in a parallel christie into the hill. Push your ski tails out and your knees inward. The down-up forward-down sequence, the weight shift to the outside ski, plus the turning action of the feet and legs together—all mesh in a continuous action. Practice the exercise to both sides before progressing.

There's another version which will help you feel the timing and coordination of the stem christie. The beginning of the exercise is different. Instead of starting down the fall line in a small V-position, start in the straight downhill running position, with your skis together. Immediately push into the V-position, plant your pole, come up and forward stepping the inside ski over to the outside ski and sink into the traverse position. Complete the turn with turning action of your feet and legs.

Common Mistakes and How to Avoid Them

1. *Delaying in the V-position.* This will upset your

timing. The stemming of the skis, both in this exercise and in the stem christie helps you get to and across the fall line. And in the V-position you should be able to transfer your weight over to the outside ski easily. This is a familiar movement. But you will lose the timing if you don't spring up and forward as soon as you plant the pole. In effect, you are combining two sequences when you make a controlled skid turn: the down-up forward-down sequence which unweights the skis so that you can easily turn them; and the weight shift to the outside ski and the turning action of the feet and legs to provide the turning power. Holding the stemmed ski position for more than a brief moment will rob the entire turn of any smoothness.

2. *Not stepping the inside ski* all *the way over to the outside ski.* If you don't close the ski, you won't be shifting your weight to the outside effectively and you won't be in the compact traverse position ready to apply turning action of the legs. One way to be sure you have brought the skis close together and parallel is to *bring the inside knee over and press it against the outside knee* (slightly forward of the lower knee). This automatically brings the legs and skis together.

3. *Not edging the skis into the hill after you have stepped the skis together.* Your turning power won't take effect and you will probably find yourself slipping sideways downhill instead of turning in an arc. When you shift your weight across to the lower ski, concentrate on being in the traverse position. This comma position should put pressure on your edges. Increase this edge pressure as you apply turning action of your legs by pressing your knees further into the hill.

4. *Stiff lower leg.* This most common mistake is without doubt the number one reason why many skiers have not become good intermediate or advanced skiers. Don't let it become a habit. You can conquer the stiff downhill leg by *finishing every turn with a down movement in both knees and ankles.* No matter how imperfect a turn you make, be sure you have completed the down-up, forward-down unweighting sequence by sinking into the end of the turn. *Finish your turns with maximum ankle- and knee-bend in both legs.*

5. *Leaning into the hill.* This can be caused by placing the pole too far away from the side of the ski making it difficult to lean downhill. Or it can be caused also by swinging the head to the inside, or by leaning on the pole for more than a brief moment. In any case, remember your objective: To go from the small snowplow position to the traverse position, in which you have a sideways break at the waist. Your head and shoulders are out over the lower ski.

6. *Planting the outside pole.* On turns to the left, put the left pole into the snow. On turns to the right, use the right pole. This is the pole *inside* the turning arc. Planting the outside pole will not help you shift your weight to the outside ski. And if your turn does start, you will ski into the planted pole.

Ideal Terrain to Practice On
A moderately steep, but short hill, or from the top of a long wide bump.

Stem Christie

What Is It?
The stem christie is a moderate- and high-speed controlled skid turn in which the skier uses a stem movement to help start the turn.

Why Learn It?
1. It is a graceful means of changing direction at moderate and high speeds.

2. It is effective on almost every type of terrain and in the full variety of snow conditions.

3. It will bring you a large step closer to learning parallel christies.

How to Do It
To make a stem christie turn you will be combining a group of movements you have already practiced individually or in partial combinations. The movements involved in making a stem christie will not be new to you. Now, you'll be putting these movements together in a different combination. The overall idea is for you to go from the traverse position facing in one direction to the traverse position in the other direction, using a small stem of the uphill ski as an aid to weight-shifting and to help you into the fall line. The turning action of the legs gives you the second half of the turn.

First let's learn stem christies to the left. Here are the three phases of the turn.

Phase No. 1: From a traverse across a moderately steep hill, stem the uphill (right) ski into the V-position. Simultaneously lower your body slightly, turn your head and shoulder uphill towards the stemmed ski, and place your inside (left) pole into the snow about halfway between your boot and ski tip.

Phase No. 2: Without hesitating, spring up and forward, using your ski pole for momentary support, and break sideways at the waist, shifting all of your weight over to the stemmed ski. Then quickly step the inside (left) ski into the traverse position, by bringing the left knee against the right knee. (Lift the back of the ski while keeping the tip on the snow.) This automatically brings your legs and skis together.

Phase No. 3: Your skis are skidding and you're in the new traverse position. Finish the turn by sinking into a lower knee and ankle position, by edging, and by applying turning power with your legs. As you pass the basket of your pole, push your wrist forward and lift the pole forward from the snow. This will keep your hand and arm in front of your body.

Practice left turns no more than 3 or 4 times before practicing turns to the right. If you practice to one side until you completely master the turn, you will invariably end up favoring that side, to the disadvantage of your overall skiing.

To make a stem christie to the right, traverse across to the left. Stem the left ski, turning your upper body slightly uphill as you plant the right pole and lower your right knee. Come up and forward on the pole, moving your weight from the right to the left (uphill) stemmed ski, bending downhill from the waist. Step the right ski closed, lifting the back of the ski off the ground but keeping the tip on the snow. Finish with a christie into the hill movement, turning your feet and knees into the hill. At the same time drive your knees and ankles into a lower traverse position in the new direction.

As soon as you have made a reasonably good change of direction to each side, abandon the practicing of single turns at a time. Begin to ski down,

making turns to each side one after another. You'll find that there is a rhythm to the stem christie that will come to you once you start swinging turns in sequence. It is necessary to practice the turns one at a time at first, but your movements are not as fluid and natural as they will be once you set up a rhythm.

The faster you ski, the easier it will be to make graceful stem christies (as long as you are still in control of the skis, of course). The slower you ski, the more lift you'll need to unweight the skis.

Common Mistakes and How to Avoid Them

1. *Trying to practice on a slope that's too gradual.* Make it easy for yourself. Practice on a hill that's moderately steep. Gravity will help you get into the fall line at the beginning of your turn, and your weight shift will have more effect here than on a gradual slope.

2. *Starting from an improper traverse position.* Review your traverse to be sure your weight is on the lower ski, head and shoulder turned slightly downhill, uphill ski half a boot length ahead, uphill hip also leading. This position is important because you'll be starting and finishing every turn in it. Get to know and feel comfortable in the traverse.

3. *Stiff downhill leg.* When you stem the uphill ski, bend that knee toward the tip of the ski. Then when you shift your weight over to it, drive the knee out in front of the ankle as you turn it into the hill. Finish your turns with a "sinking" in your legs. This will give you maximum turning power.

4. *Delaying in the stemmed ski position.* This will upset your timing and rhythm. Once you stem the

Sequence of movement: stem christie off
the fall line.

Sequence of movement: stem christie to the left.

ski and have made the proper upper body movement, immediately plant the pole. Then come up-forward on the pole and shift your weight to the stemmed ski.

5. *Not closing the skis all the way*. This is usually the result of a poor transfer of weight to the stemmed ski. A good way to correct this is by lifting the back of the downhill ski as you step it across to the stemmed ski. Concentrate on bringing the knees together. If you press the downhill (inside) knee slightly forward and ahead of the stemmed-ski knee, you'll be in the proper position for the coming traverse, with your legs and skis close.

6. *Not applying leg action turning power to finish the turn*. Your weight shift will start the skis skidding in a new direction. But it is the turning of the feet and knees into the hill, pushing the tails away, that is the more powerful force which turns the skis. Use it.

7. *Leaning into the hill during the second half of the turn*. This is most often caused by allowing the outside (downhill) arm, shoulder, and your head to lead your legs around the turn. In the modern stem christie turn, your legs should lead your upper body. This will happen when you remember to turn your head and shoulders toward the uphill ski as you stem it. Then lean out over the stemmed ski as you transfer your weight to that ski. The outside shoulder is slightly lowered and held back. From that moment on, your upper body remains in the same position. The finishing of the turn is all leg action. Your feet and knees turn into the hill while your shoulders continue to face at an angle downhill.

8. *Leaving the ski pole in the snow too long*. This pulls your inside arm and shoulder back, causing you to sit back and inside on the skis. The trick is to remove the pole as you ski past the basket by pushing your wrist forward and lifting with a forward movement. This will keep your arm and shoulder in front of your body, where they belong.

9. *Stemming the uphill ski with weight already on it*. You get a more pronounced weight shift (and more turning action) if you keep your weight on the lower ski while you stem the uphill ski into the proper V-position. Then, a split second later, make a complete shift from the lower to the stemmed ski while coming up on the pole.

Ideal Terrain to Practice On
A moderately steep, smooth slope.

Chapter Eleven

PARALLEL SKIING

Elementary Parallel Exercise

What Is It?

The elementary parallel exercise involves hopping the skis into a new direction while skiing very slowly and close to the fall line.

Why Learn It?

It teaches you to use both legs as a unit, when changing the direction of the skis. You'll also learn the timing of pole action and unweighting.

How to Do It

Take off your skis and poles. You won't use them for this first part. Pretend you have a jump rope in your hands. Pushing up from the front part of both feet simultaneously, jump the imaginary rope 5 or 6 times. See how lightly you can land. All the action should be in your ankles and knees, while the upper body remains upright. Jump just high enough to get off the ground, coming down on the balls of the feet as gently as possible. Put your skis on again. Slip your hands into your poles. Using the very same springing action of the legs, make one jump at a time, emphasizing the gentleness in the landing. Supple ankles and knees will give you this gentleness. Many skiers find it helpful to make believe they are on a surface of fresh eggs which they don't want to break. Another way of getting the feel of the lightness in your landing is to try to make as little noise as possible when you come down. The quieter the landing the gentler it will be. This gentleness will eventually give smoothness and fluency to your style.

While you are on level ground, draw a straight line in the snow with the tip of your ski pole. Standing with your skis straddling the line, lower your body by increasing your knee and ankle bend. Plant your left pole. Spring up and jump the tails of the skis away from the pole across the line to the right. The object is twofold: first, to change the direction of both skis at the same time, and second, to see how lightly you can land. Concentrate on turning the skis, rather than on seeing how high you can hop. Now try changing the direction of the skis to the other side. Start with your skis straddling the line. Sink, plant your right pole, and spring up. Lift the entire ski into the air, moving the tails away from the planted pole, across the line to the left. Remember, you're not trying to jump high off the ground but rather across the line so that the direction of the skis changes. Practice making 5 or 6 changes to each side.

Now try it while moving slowly down the fall line of a very gradual slope. Starting in your normal downhill running position, ski straight down the fall line. After you have skied a few yards, lower your body, and plant your pole. Come up and hop both skis into the air, tails away from the planted pole and across the fall line. Ride the skis in the new direction for a few yards. Then lower your body, plant the other pole, and with an up motion, spring off the ground. Shift the tails of the skis away from the planted pole. These turns or changes of direction are not done one right after another (which will tend to rush you). Each change of direction should be separated by a bit of straight running to give you

Changing the direction of both skis by jumping the tails away from the planted pole.

the chance to regain your balance if you haven't landed directly over your skis. Here's a hint which may help you maintain good balance throughout this exercise. Think in terms of keeping your legs *underneath* your body at all times. You will land in almost the same spot from which you took off, but the skis are now pointing in a new direction. If there is a sideways skidding action of the skis when you land, so much the better.

One way to be sure your legs are close together, working as a single unit, is to put a glove between your knees and hold it there by pressing them together.

The most important things you should learn from this exercise are to change the direction of both skis at the same time and the down-pole-up-down sequence.

Common Mistakes and How to Avoid Them

1. *Hopping one leg after the other.* The very essence of parallel skiing is being able to use both legs and both skis together. Practice on level areas until you can hop both skis at the same time. Press your feet and knees together. If you have to, make believe

you're jumping rope and try it again with your skis off. Then put on your skis and try it while leaning on both poles. Finally, progress to the fall line of an almost flat slope and use only one pole. The exercise is meaningless if you hop one leg after the other.

2. *Bending at the waist.* The springing action takes place in the ankles and knees. The upper body should remain almost erect throughout. Keep your head up and work with your legs.

3. *Hopping too high off the ground.* The higher you hop, the more difficult it becomes for you to land gently and the easier it is for you to lose your balance. Think about hopping only 3 or 4 inches off the snow.

4. *Planting the pole at the wrong time.* The pole action is an integral part of advanced skiing. This is the exercise to build the proper timing. The pole planting triggers your up motion.

5. *Landing with a jolt.* Stiff ankles and knees will cause a jarring landing every time. Allow your hips to continue moving down toward your feet after your skis have re-established contact with the snow. This will force your knees and ankles to press forward and absorb the landing.

98

Ideal Terrain to Practice On
A smooth, almost flat hill.

Hop Christie

What Is It?
A hop christie is a parallel turn started by hopping the skis into the new direction; it finishes by skidding the skis the rest of the way around the turn.

Why Learn It?
It is a form of parallel skiing that is very useful on steep or narrow slopes since it enables you to change directions sharply and quickly.

How to Do It
The hop christie is similar to the exercise you just practiced, but there are a few differences. This time when you hop, lift only the tails of the skis off the snow. The tips remain on the snow throughout the turns. Then, after you land, skid the skis most of the way around the turn. The hopping of the tails is only the beginning of each turn. Continue the turn after you land by skidding the skis around.

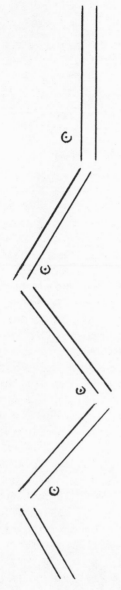

Tracks of skis—elementary parallel exercise.

Before you try it down a slope, do this preliminary exercise on a flat area. Plant both poles in the snow in front of your boots. Keep your elbows down. Hop the tails of both skis over to the left, leaving the tips on the snow and your poles just where they were. Now hop the tails back over to the right. Again, the springing action begins in the feet. The body from the waist down changes direction, but the shoulders do not. Practice hopping the tails from one side to the other until you have the feeling of changing their direction while keeping the tips on the snow.

Now try it while skiing close to the fall line of a wide slope with a moderate grade. Start straight down the fall line in your regular running position, pressing your legs against each other. Sink, then plant your pole (about halfway between your boot and the ski tip), keeping your elbow down. Spring up and forward, hopping the tails away from the planted pole. Continue the turn as you land by sinking and pushing out the tails of the skis a bit further. They will skid around the remainder of the turn. Ride the skis in the new direction for a few yards, then lower your body, and plant the other pole. Spring up and forward, hopping the tails away from the planted pole back towards the fall line. Land and skid them around the rest of the turn by pushing lower in the ankles and knees as you turn the skis with your feet.

On the first few runs don't make your turns too far across the fall line. The further away from the fall line you finish, the greater the distance you will have to turn to get back into the opposite direction. You'll find it easier if you hop the tails sideways only about 8 to 12 inches and then skid the tails another 2 feet or so. You can increase the amount of the turns as you get the knack of making them.

After you've begun to get the feel of these turns try linking them one after another with no traversing at all between. The end of one turn (which is a down sinking movement) acts as the preparatory movement for the next turn. Instead of having a down-up-down, down-up-down, down-up-down sequence of 3 individual turns, when you link them the sequence becomes down-up-down-up-down-up-down. In the middle of the sequence the down motion is the finish of a turn and at the same time is the preparatory motion for the next turn.

Your pole action plays an important part in these turns, just as it does in all advanced skiing. The pole is planted in the snow at the bottom of your down motion. As soon as it's placed in the snow, you spring up and forward, momentarily putting your weight on it to help you hop the tails sideways. As your feet come up even with the basket of the pole, push your hand forward and lift the pole out of the snow. This keeps your arm and shoulder forward where they properly belong and prevents them from lagging behind.

Another way of thinking about hop christies is to visualize yourself facing downhill, just off the fall line. To make the turns in one continuous movement, you hop the tails sideways to the fall line and slide them into the new direction. Then hop them back to the fall line and skid them into the original direction. The point is this: under normal circumstances, the hop accounts for less than half the total distance of the turn. See if you can make a half dozen linked turns pressing a glove between your knees.

Common Mistakes and How to Avoid Them

1. *Hopping too high off the ground.* This makes it more difficult to land softly, and to make a series of graceful turns. When you hop the tails sideways, try to skim the surface of the snow. Actually, you'll probably come off the snow 6 or 7 inches anyway. By thinking about staying close to the ground you will begin to feel the smoothness of the landing that gives the entire maneuver grace.

2. *Hopping one foot after another.* The heart of these turns is working both legs simultaneously. Practice hopping both tails sideways on a flat spot. Then progress to a gradual slope where you'll have very little speed (and consequently very little skidding action) but where you can get the feel of hopping both feet and skis while in motion down the hill.

3. *Not completing the turn.* You should finish each hop christie with a sinking in the legs as you push your ski tails further around the turn. As you come down, generate turning action in the legs. Springing up and forward unweights your feet and skis so that you can hop the tails sideways. Once the ski tails are moving laterally, apply the force of your legs and body to thrust your heels further in the direction in which they are already moving.

4. *Leaning into the turn with your head.* Without fail, your body will follow your head. You end up out of balance with your weight on the uphill inside ski. As soon as you plant your pole to start the up movement of the turn, bring your head and upper body away from the planted pole. This puts you into a comma position for the new direction. You should be leaning your upper body away from the hill. If you're skiing close to the fall line, this break at the waist away from the planted pole will not be as pronounced as when you're holding your turns longer and making them further away from the fall line.

Ideal Terrain to Practice On

A moderately steep hill, preferably one that has a convex contour.

Parallel Christie

What Is It?

A parallel christie is an advanced skid turn made with the skis parallel and close together throughout the entire turn.

Why Learn It?

It is the smoothest and most graceful of the turns. It requires less effort than the stem christie, making it easier for you to ski for long periods of time without getting tired. And because it enables you to ski at high speeds with full control, the parallel christie provides great satisfaction and exhilaration.

How to Do It

If you have practiced and become proficient in each of the maneuvers and exercises that preceded this, you are ready to learn parallel christies. The elements that make up the complete turn are all things you have experienced. Here you will be putting them all together in one sequence. The elements are: the down-up, forward-down *unweighting; turning action* of the weight shift and leg rotation; *pole action* to help you shift weight; *edge control* to change from edging, flattening the skis, edging the other side of the skis; switching position of the skis so that there is a *new leading ski.*

Here's how these elements are synchronized into parallel turns. You will probably get the feel of them quicker if you don't practice one turn at a time. Instead, set up a rhythm and make a series of them down the hill. Parallel turns should flow. The fluency will be aided by continuous movement and rhythm.

Practice on a slope that's moderately steep. Your speed will make it easier provided you aren't going so fast that you are distracted from your movements.

Start down the hill in a steep traverse (that is, a line not too far from the fall line), with your boots and knees touching. Before you get up a full head of steam and are schussing at the borderline of control, press your knees forward and into the hill. This action will produce the start of a christie into the hill. Plant your downhill pole into the snow about halfway between your feet and the ski tip. Keep your elbow down. Spring up and forward, simultaneously advancing your downhill knee and foot the short distance forward to make that ski the leading ski, and breaking at the waist to lean away from the planted pole. Turn the skis with your feet and legs as you put more weight on the downhill ski. Sink back down into a comma position in the new direction. Remember your leg action in the hop christie? You spring up and forward, hopping the tails sideways. Here the action is almost identical, except that you are not springing your legs high enough to get the tails of the skis into the air. Come up and forward and *brush* the skis across the surface of the snow as you slide the tails sideways. This will be a

smoother movement than the hop christie because you don't have a landing that may jar your turn. The springing action is quieter than that in the hop christie. Edge the new downhill ski firmly to carve the final part of the turn.

Another way of looking at it is this: you're in a traverse position (comma position) going in one direction. You're leaning out away from the hill. You want to get to the traverse position in the opposite direction (which means leaning out over the opposite ski) without stemming or opening the skis in the transition.

Phase No. 1: Start in your original direction traverse. Make your preparatory movements (lower your body by increasing your ankle- and knee-bend; plant

your downhill pole, increase your edging slightly so that you can get a firm push-off against the snow).

Phase No. 2: Spring gently up and forward. Immediately break at the waist so that your head and shoulders are out over the opposite ski. Change the leading ski (slide your downhill ski half a boot length ahead of the other, keeping your downhill knee bent forward). This weight shift will cause your skis to skid sideways and your turn will begin.

Phase No. 3: Complete the turn by shoving the tails of the skis further away as you rotate your knees inward toward the planted pole. As you ski by your basket, in one movement push your wrist forward and toward your body, as you lift the pole out of the snow.

To make linked parallel turns, use the completion of one turn as the preparatory movement for the next. By adding the pole planting to the completion of each turn, you're ready to lift up and forward into Phase No. 2 of the next turn.

Many people have gotten the feel of parallel turns by using this mental picture: Pretend your hips are the top of a pendulum. Swing your legs and skis out to the side from underneath your hips each time you unweight (springing lightly up and forward). The action becomes: sink as you push the legs and ski tails away from your hips; spring up–forward and swing the legs and skis underneath your body to the opposite side; sink as you push the legs and ski tails away from your hips; spring up–forward and again swing the legs and skis across to the opposite side; sink as you push the ski tails away from your hips. Your legs do most of the work. Your upper body counterbalances. Each time you push your legs and ski tails away from your hips, you lean your upper body out over your legs.

If you find you haven't been able to get the feel of parallel turns by trying to do a series, practice this exercise in which you'll be making one turn at a time. It's called the parallel progression. To do it you simply build up to a parallel turn across the fall line by starting with a parallel christie into the hill from a gradual traverse. (You have already practiced this exercise and should be fairly good at it.) Make each new practice turn from a progressively steeper starting direction, until you're finally beginning from the other side of the fall line.

You finish each turn in this progression in a strong comma position, but your beginning position changes. On your first turns from a gradual traverse, you begin and end in a comma position on the same side. As you start closer and closer to the fall line, your beginning comma becomes less and less pronounced. By the time you start directly down the fall line, you are square to the skis. Finally, when you traverse

Sequence of movement: parallel christie turns.

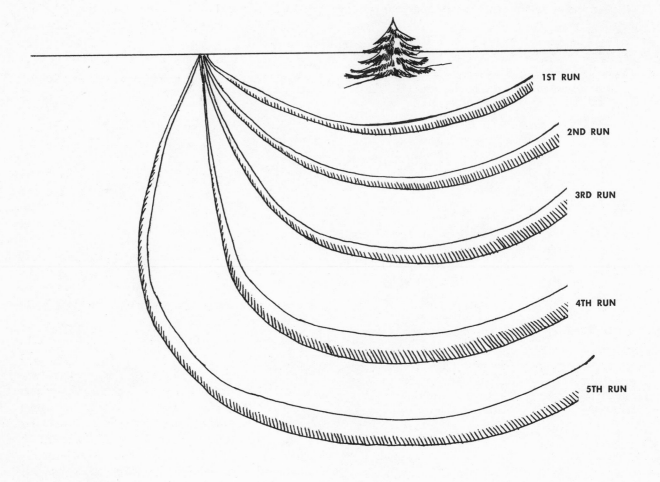

1ST RUN

2ND RUN

3RD RUN

4TH RUN

5TH RUN

Parallel progression of individual turns.

from the other side of the fall line, you begin in a comma from that side, but end in a comma to the opposite side.

Follow this progression in each direction so that you have made an individual parallel turn across the fall line to each side. Then apply the movements you have just learned by making a series of turns in rhythm. Stay close to the fall line at first and make many turns. As you get the knack of it, make your turns further away from the fall line.

Here is an exercise that will help you feel the coordination of your legs turning in one direction, while your head and shoulders counterbalance in the other. The object is to make a series of parallel christies without the aid of the poles, so take off your poles and set them aside. This means that you have to use an exaggerated down-up-down motion as well as forceful leg-turning, heel-push action. Begin by skiing across the slope in a steep traverse. Sink and shove your heels downhill, away from your body, drawing your downhill shoulder back. Punch

your knees inward to increase your edge bite and immediately use this grip to spring up and forward. Brush the backs of your skis across the snow and out to the other side of your body, swiveling your shoulders in the opposite direction. Sink into a traverse position in the new direction as you continue the turning action with your legs. Make a concerted effort to keep your legs (knees and boots) pressed together. Again jab your inside edges into the snow and bounce up from the increased traction the edging provides. Brush your ski tails back across to the opposite side while your upper body moves in a counterdirection. Increase your comma position as you sink further into the turn.

After you have made a couple of practice runs this way, try making each turn a longer, round arc turn. You can do this by giving greater emphasis to the finishing part of the turn (sinking into a deeper leg-bend and continued heels-out-knees-in turning action). Practice a few runs making these round arc turns. Then, when you pick up your poles and use them in the normal manner, you'll find your turning improved.

Common Mistakes and How to Avoid Them

1. *Not starting in the proper traverse position.* If your legs are not close together; if you have more than half a boot forward spread in the skis; if you're not leaning out away from the hill with your upper body; or if your uphill knee, hip, and shoulder are not advanced when you begin your turn, you will have very little chance of success. Review traversing. Be sure you are starting from the proper posiiton.

2. *Not sinking to start the unweighting.* If you don't push your hips lower towards the front of your boots you won't be able to generate any lift to un-weight your skis. And without the up motion, you'll find it difficult to shift your weight, which starts the skis into a sideways skid. If you're having this prob-lem, concentrate on the *down, pole, up-forward, down* sequence. Start and finish with a sinking movement.

3. *Delaying in the up position.* This means that you're losing the timing and the rhythm by staying high too long. The up motion is only a momentary lightening of your weight against your feet and skis. It is not a static position. You go up and come right down again. As you get to the top of your up mo-tion, break to the opposite side (with your head and shoulders) and as you come down, rotate your knees into the hill as you push the tails of the skis downhill.

4. *Bending forward from the waist.* What bend there is in the waist should be a sideways bend away from the hill. This puts your weight against the out-side ski, which enables you to traverse properly. Your springing action should be in the ankles and knees (as if you were jumping rope), *not* in the knees and waist. Bending forward leads to a pump-ing motion of the upper body. The usual result is that you don't shift your weight properly and you don't get much turning action. Keep your head erect. Start your springing action by pushing up, as if you're rising on the balls of your feet. Then you'll be able to use an up motion in the legs and a side-ways break at the waist to produce the weight shift.

5. *Leading the turn with the outside shoulder.* Usual result: weight is on the uphill ski and you are improperly positioned to start the next turn. In mod-ern skiing the legs provide the turning pressure. The legs come around the turn as the upper body, lean-ing away from the hill, lags behind the lower body. You can be sure your outside shoulder is in the proper position by dropping it slightly and holding it back as you lean out away from the hill. The knees, not the outside shoulder, lead the turn.

Ideal Terrain to Practice On

A moderately steep hill with a flat or convex contour.

Picking

What Is It?

Picking is touching the pole which is to the outside of the turn into the snow with a quick flicking action, without putting weight on it.

Why Learn It?

Originally used by racers only, *picking* has been adapted to pleasure skiing. It acts as a reminder to break at the waist and lean away from the hill. As such, it is an aid to weight shifting and body posi-tioning in parallel skiing.

How to Do It

Start in a steep traverse. Make your preparatory movements (sink, plant the inside pole, and increase your edging so that you have a good bite for spring-ing up and forward). Come up and forward to make the turn. Immediately touch the outside pole lightly into the snow just behind your boot. Keep your el-bow down and your hand opposite your hip but away from your body. This is a reminder to lean out and to keep your outside shoulder back. No weight is put on the outside pole. The action simulates a dog pawing at the ground. Make several picking movements at the snow with your arm only. The completion of the turn is the same as before. Sink your hips toward your toes and at the same time apply turning action of your legs. The knees rotate inward toward the hill as you push the ski tails away.

It is the timing of the first pick that is important. As soon as you spring up and forward make your first pick to the outside. The sooner the better, for it will get you to shift your weight to the outside while your skis are unweighted. And if you make your first pick just behind your boot, it will remind you to keep your outside shoulder slightly back.

Common Mistakes and How to Avoid Them

1. *Making the first pick too late.* To be of real value, the first picking action should be made as soon as you have made your up motion. If you then pick to the outside, you will be reminded to break at the waist and lean your upper body downhill.

Sequence of movement: picking action.

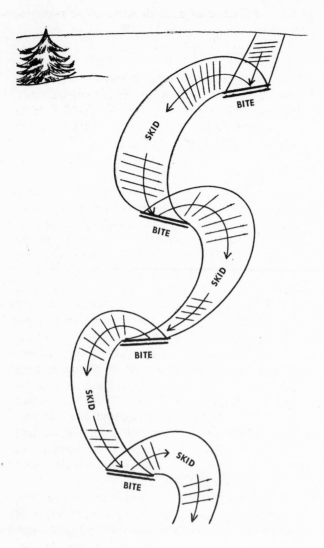

Diagram of skid and bite tracks.

2. *Reaching too far forward to pick.* Picking is just an automatic reminder to move your weight to the ski on the outside of the turn, and to keep your outside shoulder slightly back. If you reach forward to pick, your outside shoulder won't be kept back. So touch your pole to the snow just behind your outside boot. Keep your elbow down.

3. *Putting weight on the pole when you're picking.* If you have properly touched the pole to the snow near the rear of your boot you will be positioning your upper body properly. But if you put weight on the pole, you will improperly shift your weight to the backs of the skis. So when picking touch the pole lightly, but don't lean on it.

Ideal Terrain to Practice On
The same terrain you're using to practice parallel christies—a moderately steep slope.

Skid and Bite

What Is It?
Skid and bite is an exercise that leads to a style of parallel skiing in which you make a distinct parallel check before every turn.

Why Learn It?
It will increase your ability to control the skis as it sharpens your edging skill. It enables you to ski narrow and steep slopes slowly in parallel position throughout. You can use it to make turns that are not directly down the fall line in rapid succession.

How to Do It
Skid and bite is a form of parallel christie skiing. The characteristic which distinguishes it from regular parallel christies is the distinct, emphatic checking movement before each turn. This acts as a braking movement and gives you maximum traction from which to launch your next turn.

Traverse part way across a moderately steep slope in a good comma position. With a slight rising motion (in the ankles and knees) let the skis start to skid sideways. Then apply turning pressure with your legs. You'll be turning uphill. Roll your knees into the hill as you push your ski tails towards the bottom of the hill. Finish this skidding movement with a sharp drop and increased edge bite. This means pressing your knees inward and putting abrupt pressure on your uphill edges. At the moment you put this pressure against the edges, plant your downhill pole halfway between your boot and ski tip. Immediately spring up and forward and slide your ski tails across the fall line. Shove your inside ski forward to make it the leading ski, transferring your weight to the new downhill (or outside) ski. Skid the tails further downhill as you lower your hips again into the new turn and comma position. Continue the turn with leg rotation. Finish the skidding action with an *abrupt drop and sharply increased edge bite.* Your downhill pole should be planted at this moment. Use it and the edge bite to help you spring up and forward as you swing your legs underneath your hips to the other side of your body. Thrust the ski tails away.

In effect you skid into a sharp edge check before each turn (with an abrupt drop similar to the drop you use when making a stop christie). The forceful pressure on the edges provides a firm springboard or platform from which you can unweight.

Another way of approaching the edge bite is to use your legs to "punch" your edges into the ground with a short, sharp movement. Then spring up and make a regular parallel christie into the opposite direction.

Common Mistakes and How to Avoid Them

1. *Not making a distinct drop.* The edge bite is the important part of this maneuver. The short but emphatic drop at the finish of the turning skid action gives force to the check. It supplies the pressure to force the edges into the snow. This gives you a grip against which to spring up, and shift your weight to the new downhill ski.

2. *Not increasing your edge angle.* The pressure of an abrupt drop will not be effective if your skis are relatively flat on the snow. The skis have to be angled inward so that the edges are positioned to dig in. At the same time you make the sharp drop, press your knees inward toward the hill. That will tilt your legs, boots, and skis inward, putting your skis on their inside edges.

3. *Delaying the up-forward movement after you have made the abrupt edge bite.* This error in timing reduces the effectiveness of the check. The key is to bite, and as a part of the same movement, spring right up and forward. Think of the up motion as the second part of the abrupt drop. By putting pressure against the edges you set up a platform. If you don't use it immediately, it dissipates.

4. *Planting the pole too late.* As in all advanced skiing, the pole action timing is essential to success. This holds true for skid and bite. The pole should be planted at the end of your sinking movement so that it goes in the ground just as you make your abrupt check. The momentary support of the pole plus the edge bite make it easier to bounce up and slide your ski tails underneath your hips and across to the opposite side. If you plant your pole after you have applied your edge pressure you will invariably be late in springing up to make the next turn. (See 3.) Plant the pole *when* you drop.

Ideal Terrain to Practice On

A moderately steep slope, preferably one with a convex contour.

Wedeln

What Is It?

The Austrian word "wedeln" means "tail-wagging." In skiing it describes a fluid style of parallel turns all made close to the fall line in fairly rapid succession. One turn leads directly into the next in a continuous movement. The head and shoulders face squarely downhill while the legs and ski tails swing back and forth from one side of the skier's body to the other.

Why Learn It?

It's probably the most fun of all the major kinds of turns you will learn. Because you can change directions so rapidly when skiing *wedeln,* it affords maximum control with a minimum of effort. You can use it to ski fast under control.

How to Do It

As in other types of parallel skiing, you will learn wedeln quicker if you don't try to learn a single turn at a time. Try to feel the rhythm of the coordination. Although a single wedeln turn can be made, the style is essentially a flowing one where turns are made in series once the rhythm has been set up.

Keep this mental picture with you: Your body will be bobbing up and down in rhythm, from the balls of your feet. On the up movement, shift weight off your downhill ski as you slide it forward to become the leading ski. Then apply turning power, brushing your ski tails from one side of your body to the other. Your shoulders turn back against the outside of the turn, which keeps them facing down the fall line. On the down movement increase your weight on the lower ski as you push the ski tails further away. Your comma position increases (a more pronounced sideways break at the waist, knees inward) to counterbalance your heel push.

Before we go through it step by step, let's describe the pole action separately. In wedeln, the *timing of the pole plant is the same as in other parallel turns.* You plant on the down movement as you skid the tails away and use the moment of actual plant to spring up immediately, using the pole for support. But the arm action is different from that in other forms of parallel skiing. *In wedeln, both arms and both poles move simultaneously on each turn.* The hand motion in wedeln is more of a lateral movement, and the pole that is to be planted is held in a different manner. The elbow of that arm is still down but the hand is brought up and back to shoulder level. The basket of the pole points forward toward the ski tip when the pole is planted. Once the pole is planted, that hand pushes sideways across to the middle of your waist, turning your palm down towards the ground as you remove the pole. At the same time, your other hand pulls up and back to your downhill shoulder, ready to be planted on the next turn. When it is planted, the hands will reverse their actions. The hand across your waist pulls up and back, ready to be planted, while the pole which has already been planted comes in across your mid-

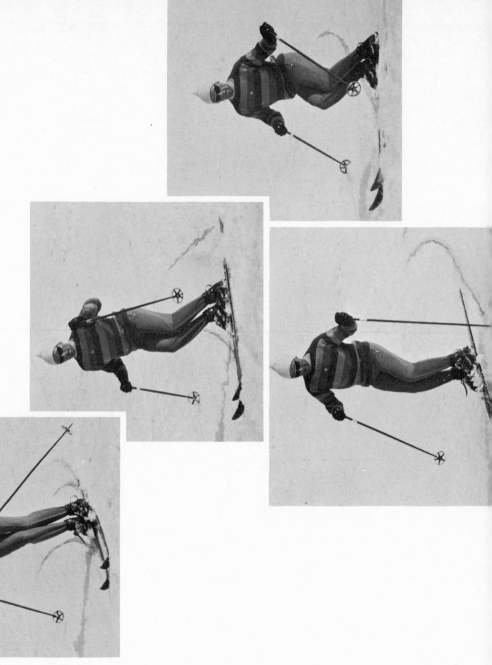

Sequence of movement: skid and bite.

Sequence of movement: pole action in wedeln.

section. In this manner you simultaneously remove one pole from the snow by rolling your hand over and inward, and you cock the opposite arm and pole by opening the wrist and bringing the hand up and back. The poles swing in a direction opposite to the direction your knees are being pressed.

Now, let's go through some wedeln turns step by step. Pick a slope that's only moderately steep. Start directly down the fall line with your feet and knees pressed together. Sink (push your hips down toward the front of your boots), and at the same time push your ski tails out to the left, knees inward to the right. This will turn your skis to the right. Your upper body swings back to the left, thus keeping

your head and shoulders facing down the fall line. Your left hand has come up and back while the elbow stays down. This positions your left pole, with the basket slanting forward and in toward the tip of the left ski, ready to be planted for the next turn.

Now bring your left hand down and plant the left pole into the snow ahead of your left boot. The moment the pole goes into the snow, use it to help you spring up and forward. When you come up, your skis and feet will be unweighted. Swing them underneath your hips and skid the tails of the skis out to the right side of your body. Your forward motion will carry you toward the planted left pole. As your feet pass the basket, roll your left hand over and

inward to the middle of your waist as you remove the pole. At the same time your right hand comes up and back, turning the inside of the right elbow forward. You sink into the new turn to the left by leaning your upper body out on the right side as you brush the ski tails further away from your body. Your position now should have your right shoulder drawn back and slightly lowered, so that your upper body continues facing downhill, even though your legs are turning out of the fall line. A continuation of the leg action (sinking lower and pushing the tails out) completes the turn.

Without hesitation, start the next turn. Bring the right hand down far enough to plant the right pole,

with the basket pointing forward into the snow a foot or so in front of your right boot. Immediately bounce up and forward, sliding your legs and ski tails sideways underneath your body and out to the left side. Bend sideways at the waist and lean out to the left. Sink down into a deeper leg position as you bring your right hand in and across your midsection (palm down) and raise your left hand back opposite your left shoulder. A continuation of the tails-out-knees-inward action completes the turn.

What happens in wedeln turns is that you synchronize down-up-down, turning action of the legs, upper body downhill bend, and simultaneously in-and-out arm action. On the down motion you push

Sequence of movement: wedeln.

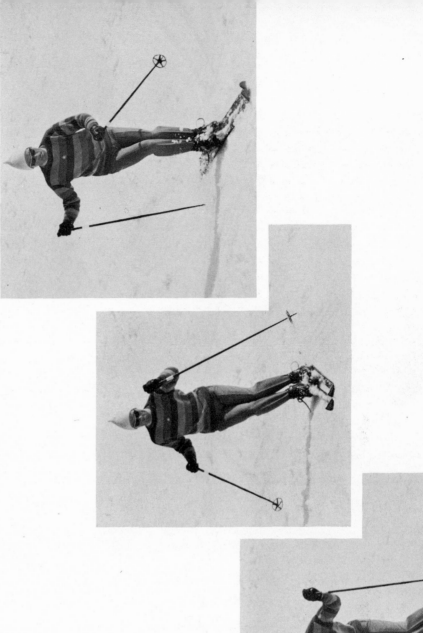

your heels out, lean downhill in the shoulders, prepare your downhill arm for the next pole plant, and bring the hand of the planted pole across your mid-section. Plant the downhill pole. On the up motion swing your tails underneath your hips, eliminate the sideways bend in the waist and start both arms moving laterally across to the outside of the turn. On the down movement skid the tails out to the opposite side of your body, bend your upper body sideways towards your feet, bring the planted pole across to the middle of your waist and cock your outside arm for the next pole plant.

Common Mistakes and How to Avoid Them

1. *Not keeping the head and shoulders facing down the fall line.* In wedeln, the upper body is relatively inactive. The legs do most of the work, one of the prime reasons it is so quick and effective. By turning the head and shoulders back against the outside of the turn at the moment you shift weight to the new outside ski, you keep them facing downhill while your legs and skis change direction with each new turn.

2. *Not sinking to finish the turn.* Since the finish of one turn is also the start of the next, if you fail to make the down movement at the end of one turn you will also fail to make the proper preparatory down movement for the next. Your legs won't be compressed and it will be difficult to spring up and forward to unweight the skis for the next turn. The secret of the down-up-down-up-down-up-down sequence is rhythm. Try it without making turns. Ski down the hill using a definite down-up-down-up-down rhythm. Every time you sink, plant your pole and come up. Then it becomes sink, pole, up-sink, pole, up-sink, pole, up. Once your pole action and down-up-down are coordinated, then add the weight shift on every "up," and a heel thrust on every "down." This blends into wedeln when you make one after another.

3. *Not planting the pole on every turn.* As in all types of advanced skiing, you use your pole on every turn. It's particularly important in wedeln. The planted pole helps transfer your weight to the new lower ski. It also helps keep your upper body positioned properly. The timing of the pole action is essential to the overall coordination of the turns. Be sure to plant your pole as the finishing part of your down movement. Then, as soon as it's planted, spring up and forward.

4. *Not enough turning action of the legs.* The real turning power comes from the sideways skidding of the ski tails. This force is generated by turning the feet, pushing the heels out and pressing the knees inward on the down movement that follows the weight shift.

Ideal Terrain to Practice On

A moderately steep slope that is long and smooth.

Chapter Twelve

SOME OTHER ADVANCED MANEUVERS— FUN, FLASHY, AND USEFUL

THE MANEUVERS in this section are not essential to your basic skiing ability, but they are fun. When added to your repertoire, they will make you a better skier. In learning them you will improve your timing, coordination, and edge control.

The first three—jump turns, step turns while running, and geländesprungs—are maneuvers you can use to cope with unusual terrain and snow conditions. These situations do not arise often. When they do, you'll be glad you know these ways to handle them.

The last four maneuvers—mambo, royal christie, flutter turn, split—have no practical purpose for the average skier, but you should learn to do them for the pleasure they'll give you.

Jump Turn

What Is It?

The slow-speed turn in which the skier vaults into the air on his poles, changes direction while in mid-air, and finishes in a stationary position is called the "jump turn."

Why Learn It?

It's a useful method for changing your direction when the snow conditions (chopped up or chunky snow) are so poor that christies or even snowplow turns are not appropriate. It is also useful if you're traveling so slowly you don't have enough speed for a christie. But the best reason for learning the jump turn is that it's fun.

How to Do It

Practice on a gradual slope that has some soft snow on top of a good solid base. With your boots and knees pressed tightly together, traverse in a line that's more across than down the slope. The turn can be described in three parts.

1. The preparatory movements are a lowering of the body into a deep crouch, putting both ski poles into the snow below the tip of the downhill ski with your palms wrapped over the top of the handles, and increasing your edge bite to give yourself a firm springboard.

2. The turn itself is made by vaulting into the air, leaping up from the balls of the feet, using both poles for support. As you rise into the air, turn your head and shoulders to the new direction and at the same time bring your feet up toward your hips. Continue the turn by rotating the entire body and the skis around the poles and into the new direction.

3. The landing begins as you straighten out your legs, make contact with the snow, then allow your body to continue moving downward. Your ankles, knees, and waist absorb the shock with the knees taking up the major part.

If you intend to make a complete about-face turn (180°); when you plant your poles, cross the uphill pole over the downhill pole. The turning movement of your body will automatically uncross them and when you land they will be in a normal position.

Common Mistakes and How to Avoid Them

1. *Stay in the crouch position too long.* In order to bound into the air, your legs must provide a powerful springing action. They can't do this readily if you delay in the crouch position. Stay high until the last moment. Then sink into a very low crouch.

2. *Placing the poles into the wrong area of the snow.* It is absolutely essential that you plant your poles in the right place—both of them—close to

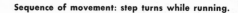

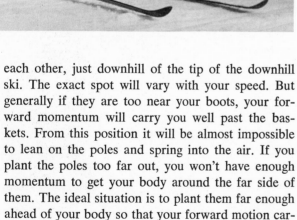

each other, just downhill of the tip of the downhill ski. The exact spot will vary with your speed. But generally if they are too near your boots, your forward momentum will carry you well past the baskets. From this position it will be almost impossible to lean on the poles and spring into the air. If you plant the poles too far out, you won't have enough momentum to get your body around the far side of them. The ideal situation is to plant them far enough ahead of your body so that your forward motion carries you just beyond them once you're in the air.

3. *Forgetting to bring up your feet when vaulting into the air*. Your turn will look clumsy and your landing will be jolting if you don't draw your legs up during the turn, then fully extend them for the landing. Finish by going into a crouch on the snow again. In other words, you're in a crouch on the snow at the very beginning, you crouch in mid-air,

and you finish in a crouch on the snow again. Your legs are extended for a brief moment when you're on the way up, and again when you're on the way down.

4. *Not keeping your legs together*. This turn is definitely more difficult to execute when you don't use your legs as a single unit. The best way to avoid this is to press both boots and knees together at the very beginning of your traverse and consciously keep them together throughout the entire turn.

Ideal Terrain to Practice On
A hill which isn't very steep and which has a covering of soft snow over a good base.

Step Turn While Running

What Is It?

A step turn while running involves changing your direction when skiing downhill, by taking a series of steps all toward the same side.

Start across in a traverse position. Most of your weight should be on the lower ski. Lift the uphill ski off the snow, point the ski tip further uphill, and step off onto that ski. (Bring your head and body directly over the ski.) Angle the uphill edges into the snow so you won't skid sideways. Bring your

3

4

7

8

Why Learn It?

It's fun and is useful. In addition to being a good exercise for improving your ability to shift your weight cleanly, you can use it to change directions when you're in difficult snow and don't want to use any of the skidded turns.

How to Do It

Use a fairly wide, not too steep, hill for practicing.

lower ski up alongside the uphill ski. Step down on the lower ski and lift the uphill ski, pointing the front of it further uphill. Step onto it. Then lift the lower ski parallel and close alongside the uphill ski. Continue alternating, taking steps uphill with the

Sequence of movement: geländesprung.

uphill ski and stepping the lower ski alongside until you have completed the turn.

This is somewhat similar to skating on skis. In both cases you pick up one ski, angle the tip out, and put weight on that ski. But in step turns you then bring the lower ski alongside, which produces a skating step-together, skating step-together sequence.

As in skating steps, your knees and ankles should be pressed forward each time you put weight on that ski. And you should tilt the skis uphill just enough so that your uphill edges grip, preventing you from sliding sideways downhill.

Common Mistakes and How to Avoid Them

1. *Not starting with your weight on the lower ski.* You'll find it difficult to lift your uphill ski and step it toward the new direction if there is any weight on it. Check your traverse position. Once you regain the proper traverse position, your weight will be on the lower ski.

2. *Not pointing the front of the uphill ski further uphill when stepping it out.* The entire change of direction comes about with each uphill step when you lift the uphill ski and point it in the new direction. If you step the entire ski sideways, there will be no turning action.

3. *Delay in putting weight on the uphill ski when stepping it into the new direction.* This will destroy your rhythm and the effectiveness of the turn. The trick is to lift the uphill ski, change its direction, and step off onto it as you put it down on the snow. It is a skating type step. When you push off the lower ski your body (and weight) glides onto the uphill ski.

4. *Catching your skis in the snow.* Be sure to lift the front of the ski well out of the snow with each step, particularly if you're skiing on snow other than hard pack.

Ideal Terrain to Practice On
A wide, moderately steep hill.

Geländesprung

What Is It?
"Geländesprung" is the German word for "terrain jump," and is a method of jumping over obstacles or off bumps while skiing downhill.

Why Learn It?
Jumping off moguls gives you a wonderful sense of exhilaration. There are times when you are unexpectedly confronted with obstacles directly in front of your skis, such as rocks, ruts, patches of earth. These situations may not occur often, but when they do you'll be glad you have had the experience and practice of vaulting into the air.

How to Do It
Try it first at moderate to slow speed. You will need momentum to carry you up and forward. But if you are going too fast when learning, you may be distracted and find it difficult to master the proper timing.

Use the terrain to help you by jumping from the

1. *Making the jump with leg action only.* Your poles are a key part of this maneuver. Plant them at the very crest of the bump and then thrust down against them as hard as you can. Don't rely solely on your legs.

2. *Landing with stiff ankles and knees.* You'll come down with a jarring jolt if you fail to let your knees and ankles act as shock absorbers. After your skis have come in contact with the snow again and

crest of a small bump. Ski straight down the fall line toward the bump. Prepare for the jump by bringing both hands up, ready to plant your poles at the crest. *But stay high in your body position. Don't crouch yet.* Then as you arrive at the crest, plant both poles near the shovel of your skis and with legs firm, quickly push down hard against the bump and spring up into the air. That is to say, thrust your legs forcefully against the snow. At the same time rise onto your poles by pushing down hard against them and straightening your arms. Tuck your feet up underneath your hips. Float for a moment. Then extend your legs down, make contact with the snow again, and absorb the landing by bending your ankles and knees, which allows your body to sink softly onto your legs.

Keep your feet together, particularly as you approach the bump. It's important that you push off both legs at the same time. Don't crouch until the last moment. Then make your bouncing down—springing up one rapid, continuous action. You'll get more support from your poles if you hold them at the very tip. But you should also practice these jumps holding your poles in the position you normally use. For there will be occasions when you'll be making a "geländi" and you won't have time to change your grip on the handle.

you're landing, let your hips continue moving downward toward your boots. Try to land with your weight on the balls of your feet (as in jumping rope). The landing will be gentler than if you come down on flat feet.

3. *Waiting too long (going over the crest) before jumping.* Timing is important to the success of your jump. Go into a deep crouch only in the last 2 yards before the crest. Plant your poles at the crest and immediately push down hard against them as you vault into the air. Your leg thrust and your arm push combine to make the jump.

Mambo

What Is It?
Mambo is a continuous series of serpentine turns where the upper body and legs are out of phase with

Sequence of movement: mambo.

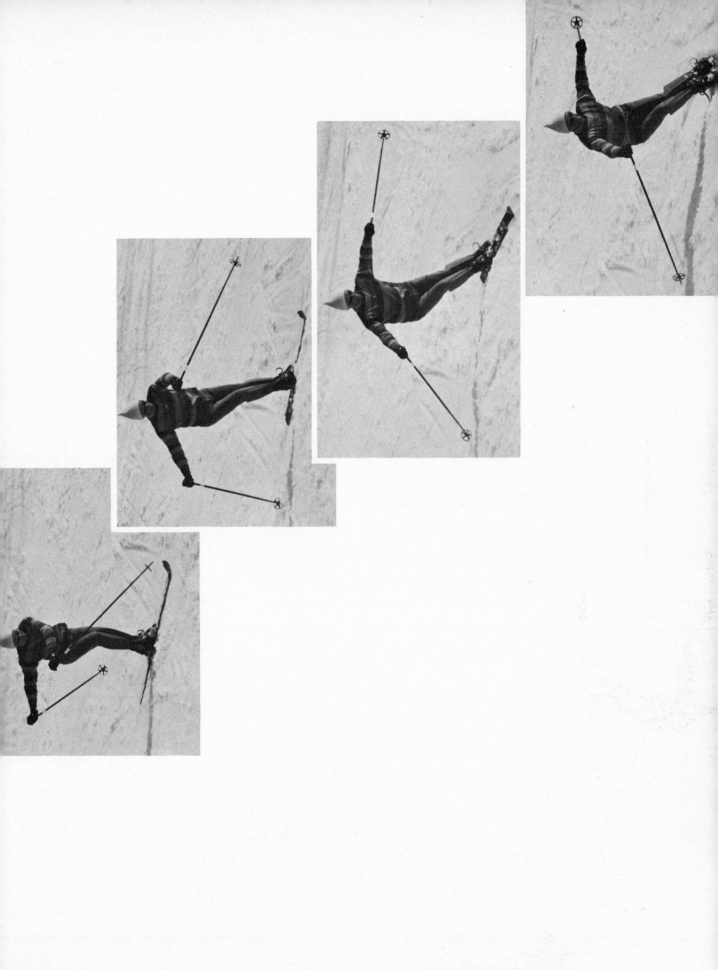

each other. The overrotating torso leads the legs around by a half-turn. It's done on smooth slopes and easy snow without planting the poles.

Why Learn It?
Mambo has no particular usefulness other than providing a curious sense of satisfaction. It's flashy and fun besides.

How to Do It
Since it was originally developed in the early 1950's, an infinite number of reverse-shoulder turns, without the use of poles, have been considered mambo. Everyone has his own personal version, which is part of the fun.

Here are the essential points to understand before you try it:

1. The turning action comes only from shoulder rotation. In fact, it's an exaggerated rotation that finally pulls the legs and skis around the turn.

2. The muscles in the mid-section must be loose so that the torso can twist independently of the legs.

3. The arms are held well away from the body with the pole baskets clear of the snow at all times.

4. There is a minimum of edging involved.

5. The legs never catch up to the torso. They are always lagging behind.

Mambo is a tricky maneuver, so practice it on a smooth-surfaced slope covered with good snow. Begin in a traverse across the hill. Rotate your arms and shoulders further downhill and around toward the new direction, without changing the direction of your legs and skis. They continue to track in your original direction. When you have twisted your torso as far as you can, straighten up in the ankles and knees, releasing your edge bite. The flattened skis will now begin to follow in the direction of the torso. Keep them flat on the snow until they have reached the fall line. As they cross the fall line into the new direction, sink slightly in the knees and ankles and edge the skis ever so slightly. The arms and shoulders now begin to swing around toward the original direction, while the skis are still moving in their first turn. The torso continues its exaggerated rotation until it can't twist any further. As it reaches that point, rise in the legs, release what little edge bite you have, and allow the skis to unwind and follow the shoulders. Hold your skis flat on the snow until they have reached the fall line. As they continue across the fall line toward the original direction, sink in the ankles and knees and edge just a bit. The skis are now headed toward your original direction as your torso swings around toward the new direction.

At the end of the rotation, when you can't twist any further, push up in the legs and flatten out the skis. They'll unwind and start to turn.

A comparison of the major differences between mambo and wedeln may help you to understand the two maneuvers more clearly.

In mambo the turning action is exaggerated shoulder rotation. In wedeln it is weight shift and leg action (heel thrust).

Which half of the body leads the turn? In both turns the two halves of the body are out of phase. In mambo, the upper half leads the legs and skis around the turn. In wedeln, the legs and skis lead the upper body.

The edging action is different, too. In mambo, there is no pronounced edging. It is a subtle action. There is just enough edge applied to keep the skis moving in one direction when the torso starts its rotation in the opposite direction. The edges are released to start the skis turning. In wedeln, the skis are skidding and then edged sharply to signal the end of one turn and the beginning of the next.

The down-up-down differs, too. In mambo, the extreme shoulder rotation is performed on the up movement or when the body is in a high, upright position. In wedeln, the turning action of the legs (knees inward, heels pushed out) is done on the down motion.

Common Mistakes and How to Avoid Them
1. *Turning the skis with legs.* Desirable for almost every other type of turn *but* mambo. To get the fluid, slithering feeling of mambo, you have to let your shoulder rotation do the work. Be patient when you practice. Mambo is not an easy maneuver, but it will come if you force your shoulders as far around as you can twist them, then with an up motion, release your edges and let the skis unwind.

2. *Planting the pole.* Your arms should be bent and away from your body so that you can get an exaggerated shoulder rotation. If you plant the pole at any time it leads you into wedeln. Keep the baskets off the snow and swing your arms energetically.

3. *Using too much edge bite.* In mambo, the skis are held relatively flat on the snow. There is a tiny subtle bit of edge applied when the upper body starts turning into the new direction but your skis continue to track. If you have edged too severely, it will take an abrupt movement to release them. This destroys the smoothness of the rhythm.

4. *Making the turns too quickly.* When you're learning mambo, you need patience. *There is a lag between the time you have rotated your shoulders*

Royal christie.

toward the new direction and the time you feel your skis start to follow around. Allow it to happen. If you try to make a series of mambo turns too quickly, your timing will be off. A rhythm is necessary, but don't rush it.

Ideal Terrain to Practice On
A long smooth slope that's not too steep.

Royal Christie

What Is It?
The royal christie is a skating-step turn made on the inside ski while the outside ski is lifted off the snow.

Why Learn It?
It's fun, it's impressive, and it's a good exercise in balance.

How to Do It
The prerequisite to making a royal christie is the ability to skate on skis properly. Can you take long, gliding skating steps where you're balanced comfortably on one leg for a few seconds? When you can do this without difficulty you're ready to learn the royal christie.

Find a gentle, smooth-surfaced slope. Skate all the way down the hill, emphasizing the glide on each

leg. See how few skating steps you need to get down. Notice how easy it is when you bend forward from the waist and keep your head directly over the forward ski. The royal christie is similar to a gliding step in skating with the addition of some turning action, which you get from rotating your entire body.

Facing down the fall line, start your second run with a skating step off to the right. Push off the left ski forcefully, to generate momentum for your turn. As you glide with all your weight on the right leg, lift your left ski a few inches off the ground with the tip slightly higher than the tail. Turn your entire body to the right. Your balanced position over the skis should not change as you glide in an arc to the right. Apply a small amount of uphill edge to the snow as you rotate your body for the turn. When your glide has ended, bring in your left leg, straighten up your body, and come to a complete stop by putting your outside pole into the snow. Then try one to the opposite side. Face down the fall line, thrust from the right leg onto the left. As you glide with your body bent forward at the waist and your head directly over the left ski, twist your left knee, hip, and shoulder to the left. At the same time lift the right ski clear of the snow (tip higher than the tail). Ride the turn all the way around the arc, balanced over the left ski.

Now try making individual royal christie turns

Sequence of movement: flutter turns.

lifting the outside ski straight out to the side. Bend the knee of the leg you're balanced on, but keep the outside leg straight.

After you have mastered the individual royal christie turns, try linking them in a series. Don't be discouraged if you don't get the knack immediately. The transition between the turns is a little tricky.

Make a royal christie to the right. As your glide nears its finish, straighten up in the waist. Bring your left leg in and bend your left knee, in preparation for the next step. Turn your right knee *inward* which will give you an inside edge bite. Plant one or both poles. Push off the edged right ski and the poles *forward* onto the left ski. Your left knee and your waist are bent forward. Your head is over the left ski. Rotate your entire body to the left. Glide on the left ski until your momentum is almost expired. Then bring the outstretched right leg in close to your body, poised for the next step. Press your left knee inward. Plant your poles. Push off the edged left ski and your poles and make a royal to the right.

Common Mistakes and How to Avoid Them

1. *Not shifting all your weight to the forward ski.* To glide in a balanced position over the inside ski, you must make a clean, positive transfer of weight from the back ski to the forward ski. You can learn this by practicing skating on skis without the turns. See if you can glide on the forward ski for a few seconds with your opposite ski held off the ground. Be sure your forward knee is bent and flexible.

2. *Rotating the shoulders only.* This will bring your head and shoulder to the uphill side of your inside ski and most probably cause you to lose your balance. When you first push off forward onto the inside ski, your shoulders should be square to that ski and your head directly above it. Then, when you

rotate, turn the entire body—the leg, hip, and shoulder. In this way your relative position over the ski will not change, but the entire unit (body and skis) will turn.

3. *Not edging on the inside for the push off into the next turn.* Without the edge grip, you can't generate much power with your back leg and you won't get much of a weight shift. At the end of your glide, first flatten out the inside ski, releasing what little uphill edge you are using. Move your head in the direction of the next skating step. Then you'll be able to edge that same ski onto the inside edge and push off it.

Ideal Terrain to Practice On

A smooth slope, not steep, that is covered with lightly packed powder.

Flutter Turn

What Is It?

The flutter turn is a parallel christie in which you flatten and re-edge your skis several times during each turn.

Why Learn It?

This is one of the best exercises for a good skier to practice, if he wants to become an expert. Flutter turns give the feeling of the subtle edge-control movements that make the difference between the competent and the expert skier. Many top instructors use this exercise when they take their first run in the morning. It gets the ankles working and it gives them the feel of the snow.

How to Do It

Practice on a smooth-surfaced slope. Make a long arc parallel turn. As your skis start turning, press

your knees into the hill in the normal manner. This gives you your edge bite. Now roll your knees and ankles away from the hill, to flatten the skis, and quickly press them back again into the hill (re-edging them). Quickly roll your knees alternately inward and away from the hill 4 or 5 times on each turn. Your edges will release, then catch, release, then grip again. With practice, you will soon learn just how much knee action you need apply to get your edges into the snow. Try to set up a rhythm for this action. You can speed it up and put in more "flutters" on each turn as you get the knack of it.

Common Mistakes and How to Avoid Them
1. *Making the release and re-edging too extreme in each direction.* You'll do better if you underplay the knee action rather than exaggerate it. This is an exercise which gives you the feel of your edges. You

have to experiment to feel for yourself the proper amount of knee action.

2. *Swinging the arms and changing the body position with each flutter.* There should be no deviation in your upper body and arms from your normal parallel christie movements. The flutter is solely an action of the edges caused by a sideways movement of the knees.

Ideal Terrain to Practice On
A moderately steep slope that is wide enough for you to make long arc turns.

Split

What Is It?
Having vaulted into the air from the crest of a

A split.

mogul, you kick your legs and skis sideways and up, then snap them together again before landing.

Why Learn It?
The split is done strictly for pleasure.

How to Do It
An easy way to get the feel of this maneuver is to try it first without your skis or poles. Put them aside for a few moments. Stand on a level area with your feet hip-width apart. In one continuous movement, push down hard against the ground and immediately spring into the air. As you come up into the air, kick your feet sideways and whip them back together again before or as you land. You have to be able to bring them back together again, so don't split them too wide apart when you're first practicing. Do this exercise a half a dozen times so you are familiar with the leg action of splitting and returning to your original position. Concentrate on making the split a quick maneuver to be certain you have enough time in the air to bring your boots together again.

Now, put your skis and poles back on, and find a small bump with an upturned contour and a smooth landing area below it. Ski straight down the fall line toward the bump. (Stay high in your body position.) At the very last moment, when you approach the bump, raise your arms and poles in preparation for planting them at the crest. Keeping your legs firm, bounce down and spring up into the air off the crest, pressing down against the poles as you thrust with your legs. The moment you go off into the air, swing your feet and skis outward. Then quickly bring them together again as you land. Absorb the landing in your knees and ankles by allowing your body to continue sinking after your skis have touched the snow again.

The more time you spend in the air, the wider the split you can make, and the longer you can hold it before snapping your legs closed. Your speed, the amount of thrust, the height of your spring into the air, and the contour of the bump and landing area are all factors which govern this.

Even if you make a small split no wider than a few inches to each side, you'll find it fun. Once you start to make wider splits, you can swing your arms out to the side at the same time you swing your legs out.

The most enjoyable type of split is the one you'll make without any planning. You'll suddenly see a bump in front of you, plant your poles, spring up off it, and split. This is sheer delight!

Common Mistakes and How to Avoid Them
1. *Approaching the bump when you're already in a low crouch.* You'll get much greater height to your spring-off if you stay upright until the last moment, then bounce down and bound up in one quick movement. You'll have more nimbleness in your split, too. Staying in a squat for several seconds before leaping into the air from the top of the bump is the equivalent of holding your leg back for several seconds before kicking a ball. If you swing it back and then forward without any hesitation, you get more drive.

2. *Swinging your legs forward as you swing them out.* This will change your body position in relation to the skis. You'll be back on the skis when you land and will not be balanced. The trick is to keep your body over your feet. If you prefer, think of it as keeping your feet under your hips.

3. *Delaying before you split.* The moment you spring into the air, quickly whip your skis outward. Then you'll have enough time to bring them together again before you land.

Ideal Terrain to Practice On
A moderately steep slope that has small bumps that are not too close together.

Chapter Thirteen

IDEAS AND TIPS

Adjusting to Various Snow Conditions

IN THE COURSE of a ski season, most skiers are exposed to the full gamut of snow conditions. Because of the generally colder temperatures in December, January, and early February, chances of skiing in light, dry powder at that time are the greatest. When the temperatures become higher, the new snow that falls is apt to be wetter, heavier, and more quickly packed down. In March, the sun rises higher overhead. Conditions will often change several times during the day. On any spring morning, you can easily find yourself skiing new snow that fell during the night. By midday it has become wet, heavy mush as the sun beats down on it. By late afternoon it is corn or ice when these exposed slopes drift back into shadow and refreeze. For that reason, adapting your technique to spring conditions can be most demanding on your knowledge and ability.

The quality of the snow will vary from resort to resort, depending upon a number of things. Altitude, the surrounding mountain range structure, and nearness to the oceans are just a few of them.

Most of the variations in snow conditions will not require any major change in your skiing. Usually, a few runs in the snow are all you need to begin to feel comfortable in it. But the extreme conditions—deep powder, ice, and midday mush—do require specific changes in your running position and movements. Once you understand the reasons why these changes are necessary, it becomes easier to incorporate them into your ability.

DEEP POWDER

The definition of "deep powder" undoubtedly varies in the western ski areas and those in the east, since it depends on the average snow conditions in each section. However, from the skiers' point of view, when the powder on the skiable part of the slope piles up to 12 inches or more, it requires different running positions and movements.

When you run with your skis deep in the snow rather than on the surface there are three resulting factors for which you must compensate. First, there is more resistance against the skis. Second, you must assume a running position which will keep the ski tips up and planing. Third, you must weight the skis evenly. On a packed slope, an unweighted uphill ski (or an unweighted inside ski during a turn) will ride along on the surface at the same speed as the weighted ski. In deep powder, an unweighted ski will drag or hook, pulling your legs into a spread-eagle.

Thus, the trick in skiing deep powder is to maintain enough momentum to be able to turn in it and to keep both skis traveling at the same speed with the tips pointing upward.

Here are some specific ways to adapt to deep snow skiing:

1. *Distribute your weight equally on both skis.* This means your body position should be square over the skis (your chest facing the same direction as the skis are pointing) instead of the pronounced sideways bend at the waist that you use on packed slopes. Your shoulders are both directly over your feet. Your upper body is erect.

2. *Hold your legs close together, with your skis parallel.* This will prevent snow from building up between your legs and skis and forcing them to go off in different directions. A good way to control this

is to try to use both skis as if they were actually one wide ski.

3. *Keep your knees and ankles bent into a deep position and your weight slightly back*. This will keep your ski tips angled upward.

4. *Keep your body upright, with your back straight*. Forward waist-bend will put weight on the fronts of the skis and cause them to dive. If you are accustomed to skiing with a somewhat rounded back, concentrate on pushing out your chest.

5. *Carry your arms a little higher and well away from your body*. This way they will provide the full measure of balance you'll need.

6. *Ski close to the fall line*. You need the speed to overcome the increased resistance to the skis. By skiing close to the fall line, you reduce the distance required to change direction from one turn to the next. The slope itself should be steep. A gentle slope, even on the fall line, won't give you enough speed to swing through the deep powder.

7. *Use lots of lift*. This is generated by pushing up from the feet. It's strictly a leg action, not a pumping of the upper body from the waist. Emphasize the unweighting action of the lift. Make it a longer part of the sequence than you would normally do on packed trails. Bounce up into the almost fully extended leg position and hold it while you apply your turning power. Then slowly sink into the deep leg-bend, and you will get a floating action which adds gracefulness and ease to your style.

8. *Run on flatter skis*. Avoid severe edging. On a packed slope you increase your edge bite in order to get a grip on the snow and to be able to spring forward. The result of a sharply edged ski in powder is that it slices through the snow. Your springboard in powder is built when you compress snow underneath the entire bottom of the ski, not just the edges.

9. *Set up a rhythm*. While desirable in all snow conditions, when you set up a rhythm and bounce from one turn to the next in powder, the whole procedure becomes easier. This is more than just a question of style and fluid motion. It's almost an essential.

10. *Be patient*. It takes a little longer for a turn to take effect in deep powder than on a hard packed slope. Give it a chance to happen.

Your equipment will play a large part in the enjoyment and success you have in learning to ski deep powder. Your skis should be medium length, very flexible to medium flexible. Stiff skis will give you trouble keeping the tips up. If you plan to ski powder often (and are lucky enough to find it regularly),

consider buying a second pair of skis specifically for the powder. If your skis are relatively stiff because you do most of your skiing on hard packed slopes, consider renting flexible skis when you do have the opportunity to play in the powder. Your ski poles should be a little longer for deep powder, since you should be carrying your arms a little higher and the baskets will sink in further.

If you haven't arrived at the stage of proficiency where you can ski on packed slopes with your skis parallel and your legs close together under control, avoid deep powder. It is not a snow condition in which you can easily learn to ski parallel. You should be able to ski parallel before you learn to ski powder.

When you do go off into deep powder, experiment with it to get the feel. Traverse, side-slip diagonally forward, traverse, side-slip diagonally forward, until you feel the resistance. Then find a wide open steep slope. The first run down the fall line will take courage, but if you follow the hints listed above you'll soon be bouncing and floating merrily down the hill.

ICE

"Ice" is probably one of the nastiest words in the skier's vocabulary. It conjures up visions of rock-hard slopes, complete with the noise of edges scraping the almost impenetrable surface. In reality, every skier is faced with skiing ice at some time or other. It may be an entire slope or only a small patch that has to be negotiated, but nonetheless, it's ice. Once you learn some of the tricks of skiing ice, you will be surprised at the amount of pleasure you can have skiing it.

These are the most important things to understand about ice: First, there is very little resistance to your skis. They are sitting on top of the surface and can easily slide around in any direction. What would be a normal amount of turning action in lightly packed powder will make you *turn too much* on ice. Second, the surface is so hard, it is difficult to get an edge bite. Checking is hard to accomplish.

If you are skiing on a slope or trail with only patches of ice (in the middle where everyone has been turning or in spots that have been exposed to the hot sun and are now in shade), *don't try to turn on the ice*. Run it straight and turn when you have crossed it and are on better snow. Usually the sides of trails will have better snow than the middle. If you are skiing a slope that is all ice, use these specifics to adjust your body position and movements:

1. *Smoothness pays off*. Avoid any abrupt or

jerky actions. Because there is so little resistance to the skis, they have a tendency to skid out from under you very easily.

2. *Turning action of the legs should be kept to a minimum.* It just doesn't take as much effort to get the skis around. If you use the normal amount of force, you'll turn too far each time and end up skidding sideways.

3. *Emphasize the weight on the downhill ski.* Although it is difficult to edge into ice, it can be done if you put all your weight on the inside edge of the downhill ski. Many skiers find that by lifting the tail of the uphill ski a few inches off the snow, they force all of their weight onto the one edge of the downhill ski and they can then grip the hard surface.

4. *When traversing or turning, keep your legs close together.* It is easier to maintain your body position and stay balanced with your weight on the downhill or outside ski if your legs are close.

5. *When running straight downhill* (the run-out at the bottom of a slope, for instance) *spread your feet a few inches apart and edge both skis a bit to the inside.* You'll have more stability in this position. Since you're headed downhill, your weight will be on both skis. Tilting them inward slightly will keep them tracking straight and lessen your chances of catching outside edges.

6. *If you are an advanced skier, control your speed by continuously turning* close to the fall line, instead of trying to get a solid edge bite before each turn.

7. *De-emphasize your unweighting.* You don't need a lot of lift to move the skis around into a new direction. The more up motion you use unnecessarily, the more chance your skis will slide out from under you.

8. *Keep your arms and hands a bit lower than normal.* This helps keep your center of gravity lower and at the same time it reminds you to put pressure downward against the slope. (This is the opposite of skiing deep powder, where the emphasis is on the up motion or lift).

Your equipment *must* be in good condition. The edges must be sharp in order to dig in. Your boots should provide a firm connection between your feet and the skis so lace your boots tightly. If there is play in your boots and you fail to get sideways support from them, you will find skiing ice an almost impossible chore.

MIDDAY MUSH

Midday mush is the extreme wet snow condition you find in spring after the sun has melted the individual granules of snow. The main problem is to maintain enough speed to overcome the greatly increased resistance to the skis. Next in importance is the need to keep your tips from burying themselves.

1. *Exaggerate your heel push and your unweighting.* It does take more effort to get the skis turned around into a new direction.

2. *Your weight should be more evenly distributed between both skis* than when you're skiing easier snow conditions. Keep your skis parallel as much of the time as you can. This will prevent one ski from sinking in, or from catching and pulling away.

3. *Use a minimum of edging.* You don't have to use a great deal of edge grip in order to control your speed. In fact, the problem is the opposite. If you edge too sharply, you'll cut your speed; and the big problem in midday mush is to be able to maintain speed. Don't overdo your comma position.

4. *Ski the fall line.* This will make it easier to maintain speed and make shorter radius turns. The further away from the fall line you turn your skis, the more snow is built up to resist the sideways skidding action. The closer to the fall line you ski, the less effort it will take to set up a rhythm.

5. *Keep your weight over your feet.* Your objective is to keep your tips up and at the same time to be in a position without being so far back that you lose control of the skis.

6. *Be sure your skis are waxed for wet snow.* The difference between well-waxed skis and unwaxed skis can be the difference between an enjoyable run and one that's hard work. If you can have your skis waxed with a hot iron, or have liquid wax painted on in the local shop, it is well worth the small cost.

7. *Check your release bindings several times during the day.* Each time you put on your skis, be certain the releases are set properly and are working. Then, during the course of the day, check to see that they are not so clogged with wet snow that they have become inoperative.

Learning Good Practice Habits

1. Master each maneuver reasonably well before going on to the next one. The sequence in this book has been carefully planned to speed your learning. Follow it closely and get to parallel skiing as quickly as possible. Practice each maneuver until you can perform it without difficulty. Then move on to the next. Don't skip to the advanced maneuvers without first practicing and mastering the preceding sections. You'll be wasting your time. On the other hand, you don't have to execute each turn like a professional

instructor before you can progress to the next section.

2. If you're not getting a particular turn or exercise, *practice one part of it at a time*. Each maneuver combines arm and pole movements, upper body movements, leg movement, etc., into a continuous flowing action. Concentrate on the individual parts; then practice doing them all together with the proper timing.

3. Exaggerate a little when you first try a new exercise or turn. By overdoing it at first, you'll get to feel how the action works in a positive, emphatic way. As you get the knack of it, you can ease up on the exaggeration. Soon you'll know how much movement or force is necessary to be effective for your body characteristics and style.

4. Work on your "weak side" turns. It's natural to practice and do the things we're good at. In skiing, this makes the gap between your good side and your weak side even greater. Overcome this tendency in two ways. First, when learning a new turn, spend more time practicing it to your weak side than to your good side. Second, whenever you come to a stop, make your stop turn to your weak side. (Hint: You can usually trace your problem back to an improper traverse position on the weak side. Practice traversing and side-slipping on your weak side. Then build up from there.)

5. Start each weekend with a quick review, making turns you have already mastered. Then begin the next section. It will bolster your confidence to have a good first run.

Skiing Moguls

Moguls aren't monsters. Despite the fact that scores of skiers, including many competent ones, detest them, skiing a slope full of moguls can be much more fun than skiing level terrain. The difference is all in knowing how.

Rule No. 1: Use a maximum of knee and ankle action and a minimum of upper body movement. The legs and the contour of the bumps do all the work. The upper half of the body remains quiet.

Rule No. 2: Plan ahead. Pick a path through the

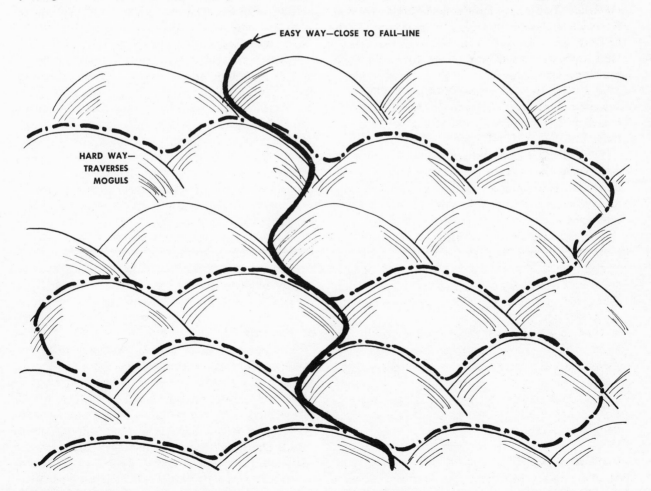

EASY WAY—CLOSE TO FALL-LINE

HARD WAY— TRAVERSES MOGULS

Paths through moguls.

moguls close to the fall line. Look for a line where the bumps and grooves are evenly spaced so that you can set up a rhythm with linked turns.

Rule No. 3: Do not traverse across the tops of the moguls, to the far side making one turn, and then traverse back across the tops of the next line of bumps. Strategically, that is the poorest choice of paths down a bumpy slope. Every time your ski tips hit the far side of the groove, you'll be jolted and rocked back onto your heels. With each bump, you'll be thrown progressively further back, out of position. When skiing moguls, you want to go down through them with linked turns, not across them in long traverses.

Rule No. 4: If you find it necessary to traverse a hill full of moguls, ski it on one ski (the downhill ski, of course). Pick the tail of the uphill ski just off the snow—this helps to keep your weight over the lower ski. Avoid the crests of the moguls as you go. Instead, ski the upper side of the groove, occasionally stepping from the lower ski onto the upper ski. Then re-establish your position over the lower ski. A picking action into the snow with your poles will help maintain your balance. Your one-legged traverse will give you a smoother ride.

Rule No. 5: Use the tops of the moguls to start your turns. The basic idea is to start the turning action of your legs when your boots are at the crest of the bump. At that particular moment, your ski tips and tails will probably be off the snow. There will be a minimum of resistance against the skis, and in that position they will turn with the least amount of effort. Because there is so little resistance against the skis, you can minimize your unweighting action.

There are many different ways to ski through moguls. Here are the two most useful methods.

STEM CHRISTIE FOR INTERMEDIATE SKIERS

From your traverse position, stem the uphill ski as you approach the mogul. At the same time, bring your downhill arm forward ready to plant the pole and sink slightly in the legs. When your downhill boot is over the crest of the bump, plant your pole, and come up slightly as you shift all of your weight quickly to the stemmed ski. It will start skidding down the side of the mogul. Step your inside ski into the lead position, parallel and close to the new downhill ski. It will take only a little turning action of the legs to complete the turn, as you sink into the new traverse position.

SKID AND BITE PARALLEL CHRISTIE FOR ADVANCED SKIERS

Skid and bite is an easier, more controlled way to ski moguls. Because the skis are not spread apart or opened at any time, there is much less chance of getting edges caught. The distinct check before each turn acts as a braking motion. As you approach the bump in your traverse position, make an abrupt sinking movement, pushing your ski tails downhill against the bump. Increase your edge bite by pressing your knees uphill. Plant your downhill pole near the crest and immediately spring up and forward, using the springboard of the edge bite and the planted hole to help you. Shove your ski tails out and away from the planted pole. They will skid easily because there is so little resistance against them when they are at the top of the bump. Sink into the new traverse position as you skid down the far side of the mogul. Complete the turn with steering action of your feet and knees.

Practicing Proper Breathing

Oxygen is essential fuel for your body. When you ski, or participate in any vigorous physical activity, you need it in much greater quantities than if you curl up with a good book. Unfortunately, the situations that confront the learning skier tend to hinder rather than help proper breathing.

When learning a new maneuver, many beginning skiers forget to breathe. They're so intent on getting the proper movements and timing, they just don't breathe. The same thing happens in situations which cause them to instinctively tense up: when coming down a slope or trail for the first time; when in snow conditions that are unfamiliar; when skiing with people they particularly wish to impress, etc. The tendency is to pull in the mid-section and tighten the diaphragm. This very neatly cuts off the supply of oxygen—and of energy.

The best way to make good breathing an automatic habit is to use the method top racers employ. They consciously force the regularity of their breathing by pressing out at the mid-section to fill their lungs, then with a noisy whistle sound, they force the air out. You can experiment with this air intake method right now.

Breathe in by lifting and expanding your chest. Hold it a second. Let the air out. Now breathe in by pushing out hard against your belt line. Hold it a moment. Breathe out. You should be able to feel the superiority of the second method. Diaphragmatic breathing not only gives you more air with each breath, but it also relaxes rather than tightens you.

Before you start each run, take a deep breath against the waistline. Then continue to fill up with air and force it out. Use a rhythm. Be noisy in your exhaling. It will remind you to continue the cycle.

With practice, your deep breathing will become an automatic habit. You'll have more energy and you'll be more relaxed.

Waxing Your Skis for Easier Skiing

Regardless of the level of your ability, you'll ski with less effort and more enjoyment if you wax your skis. Wax minimizes the friction between the running surface of your skis and the snow. Your skis slide easier, making turning less strenuous.

A very common misconception among beginners is that waxing skis is for experts only. The usual statement is, "But I don't want to go any faster." What they fail to realize is that speed is not the sole function of the condition of the running surface of the skis. Of much greater importance to control of speed are the line of descent (the steeper the line the faster—the more traversing involved the slower); the number and frequency of turns (the more turns the less speed); and the amount of edging used (a distinct edge check before each turn keeps the speed constant and controlled).

Unwaxed skis won't slide smoothly. The stop-and-go jerky movement that results has its greatest ill effect on beginners, causing spills and lack of confidence. This is ironic, for inexperienced skiers need as many things as possible working for them.

The basic rule for waxing skis is: For cold snow use a hard wax; for wet snow use a soft wax. Modern ski wax makers sell kits that include three or four waxes—one for very low temperatures, another for warm weather, plus one or two for the in-between conditions. These few waxes give you enough combinations so you can wax for any type of snow. The kits usually contain explicit instructions.

Heating the wax in a pot and painting it on with a brush, or ironing it on with a hot iron are superior to hand rubbing. More wax is put on through the first two methods. Consequently, it lasts, longer. In spring, when the snow so often is wet and slow, the paint-on or iron-on methods will make a significant contribution to your pleasure. The wax should be put on starting at the tail of the ski and working toward the tip. If you don't have an old iron or an old pot and brush you can use for waxing, take your skis into the local shop first thing in the morning. For about fifty cents they will apply the daily special, a mixture of waxes brewed to meet the conditions expected that day. They're usually pretty good.

A good idea is to tuck a stick of wax into your parka or ski pants pocket. Then, if you find your skis are beginning to stick, you can rewax them when you get to the top of the slope for your next run.

The running surface of the skis should be smooth and clean, with no areas of wood exposed before you wax them. Chances are your skis will need very little work to get them ready for waxing. Ski makers today apply several coats of protective base lacquer or a tough plastic base to the bottoms before the skis leave the factory. This simplifies your job. All of you have to do is clean off any old wax, dirt, and grease which may have accumulated and then apply the new wax.

Chapter Fourteen

RULES FOR MAXIMUM ENJOYMENT AND SAFETY

1. *Check your equipment each time you plan to use it.* It takes only a few moments to be sure there are no pieces of edge loose and jutting out, that bindings are in proper working condition, and that the baskets of your poles are on securely, etc.

2. *Use release bindings.* Test them each time before you put them on. If they are adjusted properly for your weight and ability, release bindings provide a measure of safety for you. But they are effective only if they are set properly. Test them every time you are about to put on your skis. Don't take it for granted that the setting has not changed.

3. *Warm up your muscles before making your first run.* Two or 3 minutes of toe touching, squatting, twisting the torso, swinging the arms, or climbing will make your first run more enjoyable and safer.

4. *Be certain there is a way down suited to your ability before you take the lift to the top.* You endanger yourself as well as other skiers when you try to come down slopes and trails that are beyond your ability. Know the way open to you before you go up.

5. *Ask someone to brief you on how to get on and off before you ride any lift for the first time.* Not all chair lifts, T-bars, and J-bars have exactly the same loading and unloading procedures. Don't assume you know them because you have ridden a similar lift at another area. Ask!

6. *Ski in control at all times.* This is the basic rule of safe skiing. Ski only at the speed and on trails or slopes where you can make turns and check before you get into trouble.

7. *Always ski with at least one other person.* If you should need help to unscramble yourself after a fall or because you have had a minor injury, there will be someone immediately available. A companion can summon the ski patrol in the event of a more serious mishap. If you are skiing alone and sustain a minor injury you expose yourself to much greater injury if you struggle by yourself to get down to the bottom. This is especially true in very cold weather when you can become frostbitten without knowing it. Another person skiing with you can easily see the first signs and warn you in time to prevent frostbite.

8. *Never ski when you are tired.* As your stamina wanes and your muscles become sluggish, your spills will become more frequent and dangerous. Most of the accidents that do occur happen after three o'clock, when skiers are fatigued. Don't take that last run.

9. *Watch out for sudden changes in weather.* A sharp drop in temperature can cause skiable snow to become hard and icy. Or the light may suddenly become flat (dull), making visibility and skiing difficult. Trails flooded with sunlight in the morning may be suitable only for experts once the afternoon shade has had its effect on the snow.

10. *Observe the ski patrol and area signs.* They have been put there for your safety. Never ski down slopes marked "Closed" on the area map or on slopes with crossed poles or red flags barring entrance to the trail. These warnings are there because the slope is not skiable for some reason. What's more, closed trails are never patrolled.

11. *Look up and around you before you start into the main stream of the slope.* In the same way you'd check the flow of traffic before pulling your

1

2

Carry your skis properly.

3

4

car away from the curb, be sure you're not coming into the path of another skier.

12. *When climbing, stay off to the side of the trail.* Don't force other skiers to avoid you. Stay out of their way by keeping close to the side of the hill. This is especially important if you're climbing without your skis on. You'll be creating a hazard if you punch boots holes into the part of the slope being used by descending skiers.

13. *Carry your skis properly.* You can unintentionally injure someone standing near you if you don't carry your skis in the proper upright manner.

14. *Use the special racks provided to hold your skis when you go indoors.* If you lean them casually against a wall or if you stand them insecurely in a few inches of snow, they are apt to fall over and hit other people.

15. *Don't take chances! Don't accept dares!*

Chapter Fifteen

CARE OF YOUR EQUIPMENT

HERE ARE SOME SIMPLE but important pointers about caring for your equipment at the end of the season. By following these suggestions you will protect your investment in your skis, boots, and poles. The entire process should take you less than an hour, but it will insure that your equipment is ready when the first snows fall next season.

Skis

Clean both the top and the running surfaces with a damp rag. Carefully examine the bottoms. Replace any missing edge screws; tighten any loose screws. Fill in all deep gouges in the running surface with a liquid base lacquer. (If the running surface is made of one of the special plastic materials, you can obtain the repair material from your ski shop.) The main point is to cover any exposed wood to protect the ski from moisture and possible warping. (You also want to keep a smooth running surface so the skis will slide easily.) Then apply a coat of light oil to the metal edges to prevent rusting.

Now for the top surface. If you have metal skis, apply an automobile paste wax. If they are wooden, preserve them with a paste furniture polish. Then carefully put a small amount of light oil on all the moving parts of the bindings.

To maintain the camber in the skis, stand them up with the running surfaces facing. Clamp the skis together with a rubber or leather strap at the points where they touch (near the tip and the tail). Insert a block of wood as a separator between the skis where your boots rest on them. The wood should be just thick enough to force the skis to their original cam-

ber (probably about 2 inches between skis). Don't use a separator that's too thick because the excess pressure usually will affect the skis unequally and one ski will end up with more camber than the other. For summer storage, stand skis on their tips in a dry place. If this happens to be the basement of your house, keep them away from the furnace or hot water heater.

Boots

The idea is to keep the leather in your boots firm— not soft, not hard, but firm. If it becomes stiff the boots will not only be uncomfortable but will also crack. If they become too soft, they won't give you the support they should. After you brush them off, polish them with an ordinary shoe polish (paste wax, not the liquid type). The seams around the sole need a bit of extra care. Waterproof them with one of the commercial leather sealers on the market or melt some ski wax (any one of the hard, cold-snow waxes) and drip it into the seams. Use a small amount of neutral polish on the insides. Put the boots into a boot press to keep the soles from curling. Crumple some newspaper or paper toweling and stuff it down inside the boots to absorb moisture. Then store them in a place where they will be in moderate temperature. Exposure to excessive heat at any time will dry out the leather and reduce the number of seasons you'll be able to use the boots.

Poles

Check the baskets to see that they are fastened securely. The cotter pins may need tightening, or the leather wrap-around pieces may need replacing. Untwist and smooth out the straps on the handle. Then apply a neutral shoe polish to the leather parts of the grip and wrist straps. This will help preserve the leather, particularly at the points of wear.

Clothing

Dry-clean or wash, then put away the woolen items with an ample supply of moth balls. This is the time to repair or replace missing buttons, broken fasteners, and zippers.

GLOSSARY OF SKIING TERMS

Allais technique A method of skiing characterized by shoulder rotation as the source of turning power, the rapid dropping of the upper body as the means of unweighting, while the skis remain parallel throughout. Named after Emil Allais, French World Champion during the late thirties. Also called the French or Parallel method. Once the official teaching method of France, it has since been modified.

Alpine events In ski competitions the downhill, slalom, and giant slalom races make up the Alpine events, as distinguished from the Nordic events, which are jumping and cross-country.

Angulation Bending of the upper body away from the hill, which counterbalances pressing the knees and hips into the hill. The basis of the comma position.

Arlberg technique The first organized system of skiing and teaching. Developed by Hannes Schneider in the Arlberg region of the Austrian Alps in the early thirties. Noted for its use of entire body rotation, lift, forward lean, and the stem. Has been replaced by the new Austrian method.

Arlberg strap A leather strap attached to the binding of the ski which wraps around the ankle to give added support.

Austrian method The basis for present day modern skiing, this system was developed in the Arlberg region in the mid-fifties. It emphasizes economy of movement, a more erect stance, and use of the legs in turning. Because the legs turn first, the upper body appears to be in a slight "reverse-shoulder" position most of the time. The entire body is in a comma position.

Base Snow which has settled, covering the ground so that it is skiable.

Base lacquer A hard lacquer put on the bottoms of skis to protect the wood. Most modern skis now have plastic bottoms.

Bathtub A slang expression that refers to the hole in the snow made by the body of a skier who has fallen. Skiers who fail to fill in their bathtubs create unnecessary hazards for others.

Bite To put pressure on the edges of the skis so that they grip the snow.

Boiler plate Extremely hard-packed, icy snow conditions.

Boot locks A type of release binding. The toe unit and the heel unit are sold together as a complete binding.

Boot press A mechanical device to hold the soles of ski boots flat.

Breakable crust Snow which has frozen into a crust on the top surface, but is not hard enough to support skiers. Dangerous ski condition.

Bunny A beginning female skier who is usually overdressed, over made-up, and not yet oriented to skiing.

Camber The upward arch in the middle of the ski.

Check A maneuver used to reduce speed. It involves turning one or both skis across the fall line and applying edge pressure.

Christie Short for "christiania," the group of intermediate and advanced turns in which the skis are skidded around and kept together during the last part of the turn.

Climbing skins Strips of sealskin or synthetic fiber which can be temporarily attached to the running surface of the skis. The position of the hairs permits the skis to slide forward with the grain, yet keeps the skis from slipping back when the movement is against the grain. Used for long, gentle to moderate climbs and towing.

Comma position The curved body position of modern skiing, produced by leaning the upper body away from the hill while pressing the knees and hips into the hill (or by leaning the upper body toward the outside of the turn and pressing the knees and hips toward the inside of the turn).

Control gates Sets of two flags placed on a downhill course through which the racers must pass. Used to control the racers' line at potentially dangerous parts of the course.

Corn snow A snow condition usually found in spring, when the snow melts during the sunny hours and refreezes again at night. The snow forms individual kernels.

Counter rotation   The preparatory movement or wind-up before making a turn.

Downhill   The term used to indicate those parts of the body and equipment nearest to the bottom of the slope (e.g., downhill ski, downhill edge, downhill hip). Also a type of competition in which the skiers attain great speed.

Drop   The rapid lowering of the body to unweight the skis, making it easier for the skis to be turned. In modern skiing, used mainly during the higher speed turns. Also refers to the vertical distance between the top and the bottom of a mountain.

Edging   Controlling the sideways slipping action of the skis by angling the edges into the snow and putting pressure on them.

Fall line   The natural line or way down a slope. A ball, rolling freely, will follow the fall line down the hill. All other conditions being equal, it is the fastest way down.

Flush   A combination of gates used in a slalom race, which forces the racer to make a series of tight turns on the fall line.

Foot steering   Changing the direction of the skis by turning the feet and legs. A primary source of turning power in modern skiing.

Gates   A pair of matching colored flags between which a racer must ski.

Geländesprung   A jump over small obstacles (patches of dirt, rock, bushes) while the skier is moving. The poles are planted into the snow for support.

Giant slalom   Ski competition that combines some of the features of slalom and downhill races. The course consists of combinations of gates, as in a slalom, but they are set with greater distances between them, which produces a more open, faster race.

Granular snow   A kind of snow produced when a frozen crust loosens up into tiny pellets.

Heel thrust   Pushing of the ski tails sideways across the snow, which changes their direction. For the average pleasure skier it means the same as foot steering, since the skis change direction through leg action.

Herringbone   Climbing a hill with the skis in a V position, with pressure being exerted against the inside edges.

Hop christie   One of the advanced skidding turns, which starts when the skier lifts the tails of both skis at the same time and changes their direction in air.

Jump turn   An aerial maneuver, used when going at slow speed, during which the skier makes a complete

change of direction in air by supporting himself on his poles.

Kick turn   A way of changing direction by swinging one ski into the air, setting it down in the opposite direction, then stepping the other ski and body around to it. Most often used when the skier is stationary.

Laminated skis   Wooden skis made up of many strips of wood, glued and molded into a single piece to provide strength and resiliency.

Lift   A method of unweighting the skis, making it easier to turn them, by an up motion of the body— a straightening up of the legs. Also refers to the mechanical means of pulling or lifting a skier to the top of the mountain.

Linked turns   A series of consecutive turns, in which the end of one turn is the start of the next.

Long thong   A kind of binding used by racers and expert skiers. It consists of a long piece of leather which wraps around the ankle and holds the boot firm to the ski. A nuisance to put on, it does afford excellent support.

Mogul   A large bump formed partly by the natural terrain underneath the snow, but mostly by skiers all turning in the same place. Their turning action digs a trough and at the same time moves the loose snow onto the bump.

Mambo   A series of rhythmic turns in which the skier's upper body leads the legs around the turn, producing a serpentine effect. Usually done on smooth snow conditions, this maneuver has many individual variations.

Modern skiing   A method in which emphasis is on economy of movement. Most of the work is done by the legs while the upper body, in an upright position, is used to counterbalance.

Parallel christie   The advanced, most graceful form of the skidded turn, in which the skis are pressed together and kept parallel throughout the entire turn.

Platform   A concept pertaining to lift. By checking quickly and sharply, you build a platform from which you spring up and forward, making your unweighting easier.

Powder   Snow that is usually light and dry. Once a skier learns to ski in it, he prefers it to any other kind of snow.

Prejumping   A technique used by downhill racers to minimize the effect of large bumps. By jumping just before they arrive at the crest of the bump, they avoid the crest, and spend a minimum amount of time in the air.

Release bindings   A type of binding which, under excess stress or pressure, allows the boot to separate from its fixed position on the ski.

Reverse shoulder In modern skiing the legs turn in one direction while the upper body moves in the opposite direction, or remains relatively stationary. The shoulders are reversed rather than square to the skis. The amount of reverse is determined by the steepness of the slope, the speed of the skier, and his path. Exaggerated reverse shoulder, once a vogue, is no longer the mark of an advanced skier.

Rope tow A moving, endless rope which pulls skiers up a slope.

Rotation Motion of the body or part of the body around an imaginary vertical axis, in the same manner a weather vane moves. The Allais method uses shoulder rotation; the classic Arlberg, entire body rotation; and the new Austrian (which is now the modern) method emphasizes leg rotation as the force which turns the skis.

Ruade Picking the tails of the skis off the snow at the start of a turn by contracting the legs rapidly. This maneuver from the Allais method was forerunner to the modern hop christie.

Schuss Skiing straight downhill without turning or checking speed.

Schuss boomer One who schusses because he hasn't learned how to control his skis. He often ends up in the first aid room.

Side-slipping Allowing the skis to slip sideways by making them flatter to the hill.

Sitzmark A hole in the snow made by the body of a skier who has fallen.

Slalom A ski competition in which the racer skis through many closely-spaced pairs of matching colored flags.

Snowplow A position of the body and skis in which the tips are close together while the tails are spread apart, giving the appearance of a two-bladed snow plow. Useful at slow speed as a braking maneuver, the snowplow is a position in which beginners can first feel control of the skis.

Snowplow turns Traditionally the first turns learned by skiers, they are made in the snowplow position throughout the entire turn.

Stem The act of moving one ski into the V-position, with the tips close together and the tails spread apart (half of a snowplow). The uphill ski is stemmed as a preparatory maneuver for turning. The downhill ski is stemmed as a braking maneuver.

Stem christie A moderate- and high-speed skidding turn which starts with a stem of the uphill ski.

Stem turn A slow speed turn in which skis start together in a traverse, are then stemmed into a small snowplow for the turn, and after the turn are brought together again in a traverse in the new direction.

Step turn A change in direction by stepping one end of the skis around in a circle.

Track A shouted warning which means "Attention. I'm approaching you." Also used to indicate the path or line of a skier. Sometimes refers to the grooves worn into the snow by skiers, particularly in connection with rope tows, T-bars, and J-bars.

Traverse To ski across the hill.

Traverse position The special body position used when skiing diagonally down a hill.

Unweighting A temporary lightening of the skier's weight against his feet and skis, which makes it easier to start turns. Accomplished by lift or drop.

Vorlage Forward lean of the body in relation to the skis. Used less frequently today, since the body position in modern skiing is more erect.

Wedeln A series of short rhythmic parallel turns in the fall line, characterized by fluid continuity and minimal upper body movement.

Weight shift Change in the position of the skier's body and weight in relation to his skis. This is one of the sources of turning power.